Thou Shall Not Use COMIC SANS

GRAPHIC DESIGN

365

SINS AND VIRTUES

A Designer's Almanac of Dos and Don'ts

Peachpit Press

Thou Shall Not Use Comic Sans
365 Graphic Design Sins and Virtues: A Designer's Almanac of Dos and Don'ts
Sean Adams, Peter Dawson, John Foster, Tony Seddon

Peachpit Press
1249 Eighth Street
Berkeley, CA 94710
510/524-2178
510/524-2221 (fax)

Find us on the Web at: **www.peachpit.com**
To report errors, please send a note to errata@peachpit.com

Peachpit Press is a division of Pearson Education
Acquisitions Editor: Nikki Echler McDonald
Production Editors: Cory Borman, Tracey Croom
Proofreader: Jan Seymour

A QUID BOOK
Conceived and produced by
Quid Publishing, Level 4 Sheridan House, 114 Western Road, Hove BN3 3PJ, England
Designed by Tony Seddon

ISBN 13   978-0-321-81281-0
ISBN 10   0-321-81281-6

10 9 8 7 6 5 4 3 2 1

Printed in China

Thou shall have a foreword

Hi. I'm a design school dropout. I lasted all of four weeks in typography class.

A few years ago I decided to go back to school. I wasn't happy as a graphic designer, maybe I wasn't happy as a person. Who can say? But like any self-conscious middle class fauxhemian with a *New Yorker* subscription I had convinced myself that a graduate degree would fix me right up. But those things are pricey, so I thought I'd test the waters first, and enrolled in a night class at Art Center College of Design, where I had studied years before. Unfortunately, by the time I set out on this experiment almost all the fancy classes had filled up. No 3D model making with the laser lathe for me. The one class that still had an open slot was *Basics of Typography*.

Now, by this time I had worked as an officially credentialed graphic designer for about eight years and as a paid dilettante for easily fifteen. On top of that, Art Center's night program was then designed mostly for younger students that needed to build up their portfolio to get accepted into the degree program. I was feeling pretty solid about my type skills, and downright cocky about the competition. But I thought, "Eh, don't be that way. Pride goeth before destruction, and a haughty spirit before a fall. Besides, we're none of us above revisiting the basics. This'll be fun!"

With this being the trial balloon for my return to life at the academic retreat and resort, I was looking forward to rediscovering the fundamentals with the excitement of a novice and the work ethic of a semi-seasoned pro. Instead of rushing through assignments in fear at the last possible minute, trying to guess what would please my teacher, I'd approach each task with leisurely reflection and joy. This wouldn't be client work. It'd be my little treat to myself each week. It'd be the way I had always dreamed school should be.

Of course, none of that came to pass. I wasn't taking time off from work. I just added this to my giant to-do list in the hopes that it would somehow keep paying gigs at bay. Which it didn't. So I rushed, and I fudged, and instead of learning to see old things with new eyes, I used the same tricks on my new teacher that I was using on my commercial work, too. It was just one more thing I had to get out the door.

That wasn't what made me quit after four weeks, though. I could've done it. I could've pulled through, even though the whole exercise had become somewhat pointless by now. Yes, I was going through the motions, but I was technically a student again, and maybe I'd meet somebody cute on campus. Not a trivial benefit.

But what was the real problem anyway? Was it just the hectic pace? I was used to that. Was it that I had to submit to the critiques from teachers or my fellow students? Nah. That didn't bother me. It was all very good-natured stuff, and I was better for hearing it. No, what did me in was listening to the teacher giving feedback to the younger students.

All of it was highly professional, of course—well-considered, and totally correct: Open up the leading a little. This part over here might need to be kerned a little bit more carefully. Have you considered the negative space you're creating on the page?—Perfectly good stuff. Stuff I've been told a hundred times and that I've said to people a hundred times in turn. But somehow I just couldn't handle seeing it applied to these eager young students just trying to get into school.

"Just leave them alone!," I thought. "Yes, I agree that this isn't the proper way of doing it. But maybe they're on to something! Something new! And fantastic! What would happen if we just let them run with it?"

But they weren't on to anything. They were just stumbling along, trying to get better. What's more, they didn't want to be left alone. They were there specifically to be corrected, to absorb the rules, to learn and play it straight.

Still, I couldn't handle it. It triggered something in me—maybe one too many memories of haggling with clients over one extra point of type size or a logo placement—and I had to leave. I didn't even quit. I just stopped showing up.

In the end, I learned first hand that the old saw is right: No matter if you want to follow the rules or you want to break them, you have to know them first and know them well. And that is, of course, the point of all this.

You can look at this book as a guide to avoiding rookie mistakes, or you can be an ornery bastard like me and see it as a list of "Oh yeah? We'll see about that!" challenges. Either way is good. But the fact is, everything in this book is stuff you need to know, and you're getting it from people who have proven that they know what they're doing.

Everything here is true, and to have it gathered in one volume is simply incredibly useful.

And it's a good thing that all of it is happening in book form, too, because I have to admit that there are at least fourteen things here that I've been doing wrong for years. Would I have ever dared to ask anybody about it? Hell no. Because that's the other thing about school. And life. You don't wanna look stupid. This book will help with that. A lot.

Now let's never speak of this again.

Stefan G. Bucher

P.S. While I don't want to embarrass the authors, they did neglect to add the crossbar to the lowercase t every time the word "shalt" appears. Boy, must their faces be red! If you have a few minutes, please get a suitable marker and cross those t's. Your English teacher will thank you. And me. I'll thank you, too.

Type and Typography

Thou shall not use

Comic Sans

Commentary Well, we had to put it in, didn't we—it did inspire this book after all. Comic Sans is arguably the most inappropriately used typeface in history after its first appearance in 1995. It was designed for Microsoft® a year earlier by Vincent Connare (who incidentally is very philosophical about his notoriety among type fans) to supply user-friendly menus for people who were a bit scared of computers. When it was included as one of the font choices in Windows 95, it took off faster than a speeding bullet. Everyone with a PC and the notion they could do "graphic design" started using it on their home-grown letterheads, party invites, curriculum vitaes, store signs, haulage firm truck-sides and, well, you get the picture. Comic Sans wasn't designed to do all these things, so why did every-one like it so much? Connare himself thinks people like to use it because "it's not like a typeface." Ouch! What better reason can there be to *not* use Comic Sans? **TS**

Thou shall use Comic Sans...

...ironically

Commentary Did I just say you shouldn't use Comic Sans? Well, I was only kidding. One of the great things about typefaces that become vilified due to inappropriate application or overuse is they gain a platform from which they can be used to portray irony, sarcasm, satire, dry wittedness, and so on. If you've got a dispiriting message that you want to make light of, for instance "Turning 46 next week and really happy about it—party on!", Comic Sans might just be the typeface of choice. The problem here is, unless everyone you're inviting to your birthday bash is a graphic designer, they won't get it. Using type ironically can be very effective and indeed great fun, but only if the irony isn't wasted. Therefore, think carefully before you decide to use Comic Sans, or Childs Play, or Dot Matrix, or Bullets Dingbats, or any other novelty typeface for any project that requires anyone to work out why you chose the type in the first place. If the joke isn't immediately transparent, you should probably have gone for Times New Roman instead. Ha ha—do you get it? No? **TS**

Boring!

Thou shall accept that Times New Roman has its uses

Commentary The thing is, Times New Roman is an incredibly useful typeface. It's well designed, with elegant letterforms and displays, and excellent readability and legibility characteristics. It's also very economical with space, a property that harks back to its origins as a typeface designed for *The Times* newspaper in 1931. Its biggest problem is that it's totally ubiquitous so has lost its character. Everyone with a PC can identify it, thanks once again to Microsoft, who've bundled it with Windows since 1992 and made it the default typeface for Word. It's also one of the most widely used typefaces in mass-market paperbacks, particularly in the States. This is why we graphic designers get all sniffy about using it. But are we being fair? I'm not so sure. If it's not such a great typeface, how come it's used more than any other for so many varying applications? I think it's time to accept Times New Roman for what it is and give thanks for its usefulness. But will I be using it for my next commercial design commission? No way—it's Times New Roman, for goodness' sake! **TS**

004

Thou shall not use Zapf Dingbats

....

Commentary Good design is about good ingredients. If one were a chef, the best spices, vegetables, and meats would be necessary. A bad chef is someone who chooses the pre-made cake mix, rather than making a wonderful cake from scratch. Zapf Dingbats are well drawn, and have an excellent pedigree, created by Hermann Zapf. But they are ubiquitous and "off the shelf." They work well for handmade signs for lost dogs or birthday parties. Like most design elements, a good rule of thumb is to ask this question: "Could my mother design this?" Unless your mother is a noted designer, she will design an invitation for her weekly bridge game with Zapf Dingbats. Your poster for a client such as the Melbourne Opera or the Louvre Museum deserves better. Unfortunately, while they are useful and in some instances (the triangle and simple star) acceptable, Zapf Dingbats will create work that is dull, ordinary, and expected. As a designer, one of our jobs is to create delight. Create a custom form for an arrow, asterisk, or scissors. If great design were in the details, why would choosing a banal detail be correct? **SA**

Thou shall worship classic typefaces

Commentary What designates a typeface as a "classic?" Firstly, it doesn't mean the typeface has to be a hundred years old, as any typeface providing a marker for a prominent graphic style can be considered a classic. I was fortunate to work with designer and writer Tamye Riggs on a book about classic fonts in 2009 and she came up with a great analogy involving fonts and automobiles, whereby every year seems to produce its own classic car. The same can be said of fonts—any typeface that makes a credible mark on typography has a right to join the "classics" club—Archer (as used in this book) being a good example of a releatively new font that has become a classic very quickly. The digital revolution has placed thousands of (often quite bad) fonts at our disposal, but for me it's the typefaces that have best made the transition from movable type to digitized font that are true classics. These are fonts that will always remain relevant and should indeed be worshiped, although respected is probably a better word. Use them wisely and often—they'll never let you down. **TS**

006

Thou shall learn about typographic classification

Old Style
Transitional
Neoclassical

Commentary It's normal to make type choices based on the "feel" you get from a typeface, but knowing at least a little about typographic classification, this being the grouping of typefaces which share similar design characteristics, can help you reach a more informed decision when it comes to specialist type usage. For example, the Transitional serif typefaces from the mid-18th century, such as Baskerville, are refined versions of Old Style serifs dating back as far as the late 15th century, which means they are more elegant and easier to read. Decorative or Novelty faces are highly stylized and completely unsuitable for running text (among other things), especially as there is often only a single weight in the type family. Display faces are versions of a standard font weight, often roman, that are slightly bolder in order to render them more effective at larger sizes on signage. A little background knowledge on a typeface's origins can go a long way. **TS**

Typefaces shown are Centaur, Baskerville, Modern No .216, Albertus, Memphis, Univers, Gill Sans, Bauhaus, Eurostile, Shelley Allegro, Sign Painter House Casual, Featherpen, Fette Fraktur, Rosewood, and Vantasy House.

Glyphic Slab
Grotesque
Humanist
Geometric
Square *Formal*
Casual *Calligraphic*
Blackletter
ANTIQUE
novelty

007

Thou shall not choose the latest cool typeface for every new project you work on

Graves and Sons

MORTICIANS

....

Commentary As designers, we're all susceptible to a bit of typeface mania every now and again. You know how it is—a *MyFonts* newsletter arrives in your Inbox, you scroll down, and there it is. You think, "My God! That font is amazing. I must buy it and use it on the project I'm just about to start." But hold on just a second. It might be a great typeface that you can't live without, but is it truly right for the project? More to the point, will your client respond well to it? For example, if you're working on a new logo for a

mortician, *MetroScript* might not be a good font choice, no matter how much you like it. Likewise, **Futura** might not be ideal for the badge of the local amateur baseball team's uniform, unless of course they all work together at an interior design store and are in to 1920s European architecture. These are extreme examples of course, but think carefully about the appropriateness of your font choices, and try not to get carried away by your own personal favorites when a tried and trusted font might serve you better. **TS**

Thou shall learn that trendy typefaces do not always prevail

Commentary Life is full of regrets and errors. Why did I say yes to that last cocktail? Perhaps the adoption of 12 children was overkill? Trendy typography is one of the most egregious of these errors. Curlz may seem "wacky" and "fun," but it will ruin your life. As designers, we have the pressure of remaining aware of shifts in popular culture. Understanding what is trendy is part of the job. The obvious reason for choosing classic over trendy typefaces is that the trendy fonts will soon be out of style. Classic fonts have survived the test of time. Consider your haircut in high school. Is that school photo one that you use as your headshot for publications? No. Each of us, at one point, has fallen into a trendy and tragic hairstyle. Trendy type is the same. Template Gothic was groundbreaking in 1990. Four years later, all of these projects were dismissed as, "So 1990." These projects now sit unseen in designers' flat files, like a high school senior photo, hidden from public view. **SA**

009

Thou shall accept that legibility and readability are more important than typographic styling

Commentary Our purpose as designers is to communicate effectively, but the number of options available to us can often be beguiling. To start with, an array of typographic stylings can be applied to a headline or a body of text; designers often submit text matter that has numerous styles (we jokingly refer to this type of designer in my studio as a "Ten-Typeface-Terry"—apologies to Terrys everywhere!). Sadly, this approach not only makes it very hard for the reader to navigate their way through and understand the content of the text, it is also nasty on the eye and makes for an unpleasant reading experience. I always turn the page if it appears typographically confusing— if the audience decides to do the same, then the designer has failed in their task to provide legibility and readability. Keep it simple, choose appropriately, and respect the words. **PD**

Thou shall throw legibility and readability out of the window

Commentary Legibility and readability are not always of utmost importance. You only have to look at the hugely influential body of work created by David Carson during the 1990s when he was art director of *Raygun* magazine—an era that pioneered what later became known as "grunge" typography. Typography influenced by this style was often practically illegible, relying on the visual impact of the type to convey the core meaning of the layout. Admittedly, much of the work produced during that period now looks dated but, graphically, much of it also still looks spectacular, almost more art than graphic design. Where does art end and graphic design begin, though—there's a good question. The bottom line is, if you're designing a public service leaflet for a government department or a book about Swiss furniture design, grunge typography really isn't the way to go. However, if your audience is likely to respond to typography that is a little more radical, legibility and readability may indeed be heading for the sidewalk. **TS**

Thou shall learn about the anatomy of letterforms

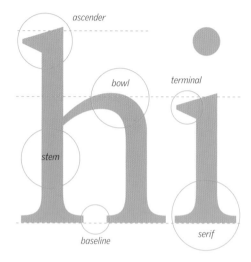

ascender

bowl

terminal

stem

baseline

serif

Commentary I've always been fascinated by how many intriguing terms there are for the components that make up letterforms: ascenders, balls, chins, dots, and so on. Any designer worthy of the name should really spend time learning the names of these components that make up characters. You'll find it most useful when it comes to choosing typefaces for a design as you'll understand how the individual letterforms are constructed and will be able to compare particular typefaces with an "expert" eye. This is particularly important when considering which typeface to use as text matter; you can use this knowledge to help evaluate the appropriateness and legibility of a typeface. If you decide to take on the challenge of designing your own typeface, it's even more important that you know about the anatomy of letterforms and how these elements have an effect on a typeface's appearance and structure. **PD**

011

012

Thou shall
learn about
the anatomy
of letterforms

Thou shall avoid using
Truetype fonts when
making PDFs for print

Commentary I've always been fascinated by how many intriguing terms there are for the components that make up letterforms: ascenders, balls, chins, dots, and so on. Any designer worthy of the name should really spend time learning the names of these components that make up characters. You'll find it most useful when it comes to choosing typefaces for a design as you'll understand how the individual letterforms are constructed and will be able to compare particular typefaces with an "expert" eye. This is particularly important when considering which typeface to use as text matter; you can use this knowledge to help evaluate the appropriateness and legibility of a typeface. If you decide to take on the challenge of designing your own typeface, it's even more important that you know about the anatomy of letterforms and how these elements have an effect on a typeface's appearance and structure. **PD**

Commentary It would be incorrect to state that you can't use TrueType fonts to generate PDF files in a print workflow—it wouldn't be true. What I'm saying is, if you can avoid using them, do so. A few years ago, embedding TrueType fonts in a PDF was a bigger issue and sometimes fonts wouldn't output to RIPs or laser writers correctly, instead reverting to default fonts like Courier. Bear in mind that the PDF format grew out of postscript so in the early days of digital there existed a kind of "built-in" preference for postscript fonts. Fortunately, things have improved a great deal since then but glitches can still occur if your chosen output device doesn't want to play ball. If you absolutely must use your favorite TrueType font and do experience output issues, there's a workaround. You can use Acrobat to export a PDF to Postscript then redistill the file back to PDF, thus converting all embedded fonts to the Postscript format. Or you can avoid TrueType fonts and save yourself the hassle. **TS**

Commentary It would be incorrect to state that you can't use TrueType fonts to generate PDF files in a print workflow—it wouldn't be true. What I'm saying is, if you can avoid using them, then do so. A few years ago, embedding TrueType fonts in a PDF was a bigger issue and sometimes fonts wouldn't output to RIPs or laser writers correctly, instead reverting to default fonts like Courier. Bear in mind that the PDF format grew out of Postscript, so in the early days of digital there existed a kind of "built-in" preference for

Postscript fonts. Fortunately, things have improved a great deal since then but glitches can still occur if your chosen output device doesn't want to play ball. If you absolutely must use your favorite TrueType font and do experience output issues, there's a workaround. You can use Acrobat to export a PDF to Postscript, and then redistill the file back to PDF, thus converting all embedded fonts to the Postscript format. Or you can avoid TrueType fonts and save yourself the hassle. **TS**

013

Thou shall not use "free" fonts unless you are sure they are of good quality

100% FREE!*

* No guarantee of quality or usability

Commentary In the last few years, there has been an explosion in the number of typefaces the designer can choose from. This is thanks to the development of relatively easy-to-use typeface creation software and the rise of websites dedicated to the sharing or selling of typefaces. Many of the typefaces are available online to download free of charge or for a nominal fee. However, on a number of occasions, my studio has found that "free" fonts don't work as they should; whether on a printout, in a PDF, or within live files sent to an editor, they have either failed to display properly or they do not work at all. This has obviously created great difficulties because, by that stage, the design has been established, refined, and approved—the only solution is to find a replacement typeface. If there is a deadline to meet (and there always is!), this can cause tension between yourself and the client. Always check the typeface's integrity and make sure it works as it should before incorporating it into your design. **PD**

Verdana

Times New Roman

Arial

Palatino

Courier

Tahoma

Trebuchet

Georgia

Lucida

Thou shall not design for print using system fonts

Commentary System fonts are made for civilians. These are basic choices provided to everyone so websites will download correctly, and so a child can make a sign for their bedroom door. Some system fonts, such as Times Roman and Helvetica, are beautiful typefaces. Times Roman was designed for *The Times* in 1931, and Helvetica was designed in 1957. They are legible, clear, and refined. Unfortunately, they are everywhere. And anything that is everywhere becomes background noise or wallpaper that we do not see. Telephone poles are a good example.

They are everywhere, but we don't see them. Now there are exceptions. Arial and Georgia are system fonts, that are good choices for websites. They are poor choices for printed materials, or instances where you need a distinctive voice. "But Verdana is perfectly fine," you may say. And yes, it is. But so is raw concrete. I'd rather choose another surface for my house. It is important to have a broad and deep knowledge of typefaces. Recognizing a refined cut of Univers as opposed to system Verdana is what separates a good designer from those designing telephone book ads. **SA**

015

Typography Today

§

1800-1850
The Fann Street Foundry

British typeface design and its lasting influence on American typographic culture.

Thou shall mix typeface choices to create typographic texture

Commentary Different typefaces don't always work together naturally, but good combinations of fonts from opposing type families can create wonderful typographic texture. For an experienced typographer, the process is largely intuitive and, let's face it, everyone is going to have their own opinion about which typefaces combine well. However, it's useful to have a few ground rules to follow. Firstly, look for historical links between typefaces and try combinations where the features of each font underpin their role in your layout; for example, an early grotesque for headlines with an elegant transitional serif for the text. Secondly, look at the proportions of different typefaces and select font combinations where there's a harmonious link between, say, character heights and widths. Thirdly, try to pick up on any qualities that different typefaces might share, such as elegant stems and bowls, consistent stroke thickness, and so on. The important thing is to identify exactly what part each font has to play in the layout and take care to stick to the plan. If you don't, you'll end up with typographic soup. **TS**

3 VACATIONS FOR THE PRICE OF 1!!

This vacation package includes:

a **4 day** and **3 night**

CARRIBEAN CRUISE

and scuba diving excursion

Meals and Entertainment included!!

5 days and 4 nights in Orlando plus:

3 days and **2 nights** in

Puerto Rico

5 days and 4 nights in Orlando plus:

Only $299.99 per person!

Includes roundtrip airfare for two!!

1-888-123-4567

Thou shall not mix typefaces to create hierarchy

Commentary Postcards for raves and nightclubs are a wonderful cacophony of typography, color, and sparkly objects. "Look at me! Look over here! No, look here!" they shout. It's great fun until one needs to find an address. Many designers make the error of trying to create hierarchy using similar techniques. This leads to solutions that are confusing, chaotic, and desperate. Desperation is not pretty in a singles bar, and it's not pretty in design. Creating clear hierarchy is an exercise in patience and restraint.

❀ Choose one typeface for body copy

❀ Choose a size

❀ Choose a color

❀ Choose a weight

❀ Choose a case style

Now for the headline: change one attribute, and only one. Change the weight, size, color, or case. Then stop. Do not change the typeface, add a color, make the headline larger, or use all caps. That is good for race postcards; nor is ir good for clear information. **SA**

Thou shall not mix serif fonts in a layout

Commentary Few people can manage mixing stripes and plaids. Edward, the Prince of Wales, managed to mix plaids and plaids, but he had hours of free time to perfect this, and when you're quite rich, everyone assumes you must be correct. When one of us attempts the same, we look like a character from a barbershop quartet. This is why mixing serif fonts can be disturbing. I'm talking here about mixing serif fonts, such as Garamond with Bembo. They are both beautiful typefaces, but they are too similar. If you are designing a publication to be read by an educated group of typophiles, they may say, "Isn't that ironic?" The rest of us will only find something that looks as if the designer made a mistake, or the proofreader wasn't paying attention. This will render the same response as when we see someone mixing plaids, "That's just sad and wrong." **SA**

Thou shall not use ultra thin typefaces for logo design

Commentary There are times when a client requests something that defies the laws of physics. They may request larger type and additional copy in a smaller space. Or, they may ask for a logo with ultra thin letterforms. Most logos will be reduced to fit on a business card, or in the corner of a website. The laws of physics dictate that a thin typestyle will be thinner when reduced in scale. If a logo is made with ultra thin letterforms, at some point these letterforms will be as thin as a single atom. No printer will be able to print this, and nobody will see it. The solution is to create logos that can be scaled to a small size and remain clear. Additionally, good logos are strong and confident. No company or organization should be portrayed as being weak, ineffectual, and anemic. **SA**

019

Thou shall always choose a typeface with an acceptable range of weights for body text

Arno Pro Regular // *Italic* // **Semibold** // ***Semibold Italic*** // **Bold** // ***Bold Italic*** // Light Display // *Light Italic Display* // Caption // SmText // Subhead // Display // *Italic caption* // *Italic SmText* // *Italic Subhead* // *Italic Display* // **Semibold Caption** // **Semibold SmText** // **Semibold Subhead** // **Semibold Display** // ***Semibold Italic Caption*** // ***Semibold Italic SmText*** // ***Semibold Italic Subhead*** // ***Semibold Italic Display*** // **Bold Caption** // **Bold SmText** // **Bold Subhead** // **Bold Display** // ***Bold Italic Caption*** // ***Bold Italic SmText*** // ***Bold Italic Subhead*** // ***Bold Italic Display***

Commentary When you need to typeset any amount of body text, please be sure to select a typeface with at least a couple of weights in both roman and bold, and more importantly, one with proper italics. It's a surprisingly common mistake for designers to choose a font based purely on its looks (not a bad thing *per se*, so don't shout me down here) but with little or no consideration for its versatility. Imagine the scenario: The presentation is completed and the "industrial" theme looks wonderful with DIN 1451 as the text font, then the editor calls you up to say, "I want to introduce italics in the running text. How can I do that with this font?" Disaster; there are no italic weights, and don't you dare add a slant to the roman font! Okay, you could switch to the DIN Open Type collection, which has lots of italic weights, but if you don't already own it and the client insists they like the typeface you've used, you've got an unexpected expense against the project's budget. Serves you right! **TS**

Now, this does seem like a bit of **overkill**. The more I think about it, chances are that we could have managed with one font. Don't you think?

Hello? Anyone home?

Anyone?

Thou shall not use any more typefaces in one layout than is absolutely necessary

---

Commentary This is one rule that leaves a little ambiguity. However, a solid gauge is that as soon as you notice that a layout has a lot of fonts, it probably has too many. If we all take an honest approach, we can admit that we rarely need more than one sans-serif and one serif font to complete most assignments. Holding to typefaces that have full sets so that we have usable bold, italics, and whatnot, will bring most any document to fruition.

If you find your designs using different fonts for the introductory paragraph, drop cap, caption, folio, body copy, pull quote—well, then you have six typefaces in action already, along with a confused reader, and we haven't even talked about headlines. Give me back four of the fonts and let's try this again. You'll thank me later. **JF**

From the freeway, take the second exit for Pepper Lake which you reach by following the road for approximately three miles. Just before you reach Pepper Lake itself, take the small road to your right next to the Tourist Information building. Follow the road for approximately two miles until you come to a fork, take the left hand fork and drive for another 400 yards until you reach the clearing where the wedding ceremony will take place. See you on Saturday!

Thou shall not set body copy using a script typeface

Commentary *Have you ever tried to read a block of running text set in a florid script typeface?* I repeat, have you ever tried to read a block of running text set in a florid script typeface? It's hard work, isn't it, and explains why designers in-the-know tend not to make that type choice. I've racked my brains trying to think of a situation where you might want to do this, and with the possible exception of a wedding invitation I really can't think of one. In fact, I can't think of a good reason to use a script font for the text on a wedding invitation either if you expect any of the guests to actually read it. I'm sounding very antiscript here, which I'm not, but for important text that needs to be read easily and understood clearly, scripts aren't a good choice. Do use scripts for flamboyant headlines, highly characterful logos, or elegant branding, but not for the directions to the church, or your client may find that nobody turns up on the big day. **TS**

Thou shall manually kern script fonts

-170   -2   -4   -1   -4

Commentary When you do find an occasion to use a script typeface (you see—I'm not completely antiscript) it's important to pay close attention to the kerning as, invariably, several character pairs will need manual adjustment. Script typefaces evolved from the formal handwriting styles of the 17th century and many of the characters feature strokes that join them to the next letter in a word. The kerning pairs built into every typeface when it's created will take care of some, but not all, instances where, for example, a lowercase "e" precedes an "n," or a

"p" precedes an "r." The adjustments are often tiny but will make all the difference to the elegant flow of your type, particularly at large point sizes, where even the slightest misalignment will be clearly visible. By the way, if you're using Adobe InDesign®, don't be tempted to use the "optical" setting for kerning with a script font. It works well for most classifications of typeface, but for scripts you should stick with "metrics" for the best results. **TS**

023

Thou shall not set body copy in a novelty typeface

Commentary I turned to my trusty *Oxford English Dictionary* (read *Webster's* if you're in the States) where "novelty" is defined as "a decorative or amusing object relying for its appeal on the newness of its design." It also uses the word "strangeness," which for me is the more appropriate explanation for the unsuitability of novelty typefaces for text setting. To be fair, there is a place in the design world for novelty typefaces and some clients might love the idea of an entire brochure set in Jokerman. When used appropriately, *good* novelty typefaces can work, but it takes a good eye and a measured judgment on the part of the designer to get it right. I know I'm sounding like a terrible type snob here but it's true— believe me. As for setting body copy in a novelty typeface, it breaks all the rules of legibility and readability (and taste, quite frankly), so if you want to be taken seriously as a typographer, don't go there. **TS**

Thou shall not use display fonts for body copy

Commentary To explain this rule we must first establish the definition of a "display" typeface and understand how this differs from other fonts. In essence, "display" refers to the use of type at large sizes, such as 72pt size, which may be used for titles on a magazine or headlines in a newspaper. As such, display fonts are "cut" differently because they do not have to contend with being printed small. An important difference might be the removal from display faces of "ink traps" (indents in and around the corners of the letter strokes), which are used in typefaces to compensate for overinking when printed and therefore helping to retain the letterform's integrity. If you use a display face at smaller sizes you run the risk of overinking at the printing stage, and thus changing the letterform's appearance. In addition, many display typefaces only appear in uppercase and have a limited character set. **PD**

025

Thou shall use real handwriting for convincing handwritten text

Commentary Organic design that showcases the unique handwork of the designer is something magical. It is one of the very few times that only you can provide a specific solution for the client in question. This appeal has led to a proliferation of fake hand-written typefaces. They look like a perfect solution, or at least a quick fix, when seen in a catalog or on a website, yet in practice, they are far less convincing. The key to handwritten type is that it is one-of-a-kind. You know what's not one-of-a-kind? A font that anyone can have for a couple of coins; or worse, freeware that is the hacked together scribbles of a first-time fontographer. What's the harm, you say? Well, just look at a word with the letter "e" in it three times and see how it compares to the nuances in your own handwriting. Your "e" never quite looks the same. The font never changes. And everyone knows the difference. **JF**

Thou shall use ligatures if your choice of typeface accommodates them correctly

Commentary To enhance your typographic skills and to improve your work, the employment of ligatures should be a consideration in your designs when setting large volumes of text. This is not law by any means, but an addition whereby the reader and your work benefit. Where characters share a common design feature, they can be replaced by a single character, a ligature. (For example, an "**f**" followed by an "**i**" is replaced by "**fi**.") Ligatures enhance the reading experience by improving legibility and also help to make the typesetting more attractive. Not all typefaces possess ligatures but many serif families do. Some OpenType® families may have additional, "discretionary" ligatures, which can include other character pairs, such as "ct," "st," and "cp." When considering a typeface, check what is available within the character set and compare this against other families to determine which gives you the most options. **PD**

Thou shall not slope a roman font to create an italic font

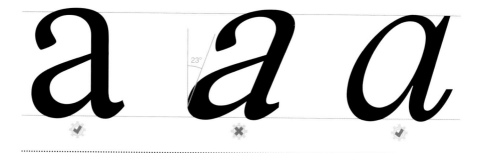

Commentary I'm always amazed when a designer takes a word and, having set it in a roman cut of a typeface, then forces it to be italic by sloping it at an angle using the DTP software. This, of course, is not a true italic, but merely a word leaning over. A giveaway for spotting that this has been done is the fact that no lowercase italics possess a double-story "a." Although true italics retain many of the core typeface's design principles, they also include changes to each letter's strokes. When a character is forced over, however, it displays none of these alterations in the letterform. With italic, a more hand-drawn, cursive approach is evident, with some of the characters linking together and more ligatures being incorporated into the cut. There is no need to "slope;" with the wealth of typefaces available, a good typeface family will contain italic versions of most, if not all roman weights. **PD**

Thou shall not falsely embolden fonts to create bold weights

Commentary Just as you shouldn't "slope" a roman typeface to make it appear italic (because it isn't true to the typeface's design), lighter weights shouldn't be adjusted to make them appear bolder. Doing this is not only unnecessary (just pick a typeface that has a variety of weights instead), it also increases the size of the letterform by placing a border around it, therefore knocking it out of alignment with the rest of the text on the baseline, x-height, and cap-height rules.

Distorting the design of the letterform means it loses its inherent personality. You will find that the counters and serifs fill in and become "bloated" in appearance. DTP and illustration packages do allow you to apply a stroke around words, but it is a rather lazy approach and for the reasons described above is poor design practice. There are stylistic exceptions to the rule, such as when applying outlines to headlines or titles, but, for text matter, use a bold variant and don't falsely embolden. **PD**

029

Thou shall reward typefaces that work well as body copy with long-term commitments

I ♥ Trade Gothic

Commentary When you first start out as a professional, you find yourself drawn to numerous relationships, all with certain benefits (and drawbacks). Some may be mentoring alliances, with long-term benefits, while others carry the thrill of a whirlwind romance. As we grow into our later years, we find we are drawn to relationships that provide stability and reliability. Someone who shows up on time and always pays their bill at the bar. Later still, we notice that some people are not only the rocks in our stormy seas, but they strive to make us look better than we actually are, and often times, they succeed. It may not have the rush of the new romance, but it is far more fulfilling. If we have any sense whatsoever, we marry ourselves to these people (professionally or otherwise). You do know we are talking about typefaces, right? **JF**

Thou shall not buy into the twelve good typefaces theory

Commentary The great designer Massimo Vignelli is arguably the most prominent champion of the theory that you only need twelve good typefaces. Now, I'm a massive fan of Vignelli's work. He designed the New York subway map and the iconic American Airlines logo, and his work for Knoll during the 1970s still informs the company's work to this day. Despite all this, I can't agree with him on this one. It's true to an extent that we now have so many thousands of typefaces because type design as an industry continues to produce typefaces as commercial products. It's also true that thousands of those typefaces are pretty awful and practically unusable. However, there are of course more than twelve good typefaces. The important point to make here is that a typeface choice is about appropriateness as well as the design of the typeface itself. We no longer have to restrict ourselves to the narrow selection that was available to typographers in the 16th century— so why do it? By all means, build a selective catalog of typefaces you favor, but don't stop at twelve, and never stop searching for perfection. **TS**

Thou shall increase a serif font's italics by ½pt in body copy

Read *Book Title*

24pt

Read *Book Title*

24pt   24.5pt

Yes

Commentary Gustave Flaubert said, "Le bon Dieu est dans le détail." This roughly translates to "God is in the details." Part of being a good designer is having the ability to think in broad strokes, and simultaneously, being detail-oriented. In some instances, an italic font has been created artificially by simply slanting the roman version. This is a sin. True serif italic fonts are completely unique letterforms, distinct from the roman version. They may be thinner and smaller optically than their roman companion. The type may be uniformly set as 8pt Garamond with roman and italic words, but the italics will look smaller. You can ignore this and state that you are a purist and all type should be left to their original size, but that would be lazy. A good option to solve this optical problem is to increase the serif italic copy by $1/2$pt. In headline situations, the size adjustment should be explored optically. The fine details in the craft of typography help a project transcend the ordinary to become spectacular. **SA**

Thou shall optically adjust point sizes in mixed serif and sans-serif body copy

8pt — I'm not burying my head in the sand and I understand the challenges and problems we face. As Jack Kennedy said, "We do these things not because they are easy, but because they are hard." We need to use our talents to solve our problems with smart dialogue and good old-fashioned action.

8pt — I'm not burying my head in the sand and I understand the challenges and problems we face. As Jack Kennedy said, "We do these things not because they are easy, but because they are hard." We need to use our talents to solve our problems with smart dialogue and
7pt — good old-fashioned action. **Yes**

Commentary Similar to the optical issues of roman and italic serif fonts, mixing sans-serif typefaces with serif typefaces requires optical adjustment. Serif fonts have changing thick and thin line weights in each character. Their overall proportion is meant to work well as body copy. Sans-serif fonts have fairly consistent line weights within each character. Their x-height is often slightly larger than a serif font. If using a mixture of sans-serif and serif fonts within the same headline, or body text, adjust the size of the sans-serif to optically match the serif. This usually requires a slight reduction in the size of the sans-serif font. If ignored, the viewer will read the copy and see the optically larger sans-serifs words as shouting over the other copy. It is rare that this is the author's intent unless the text is accusatory and angry. **SA**

Thou shall use old-style figures with U&L typography

August 15, 2011
Aligning Figures

August 15, 2011 ← Yes
Old-style Figures

Commentary Years ago a designer received typewritten pages from his or her client. A typesetter took these pages and typeset the copy. Good typesetters were masters of fine detail. Today, designers have taken on the task of typesetting, and the responsi-bility to maintain the same high standards of quality has changed hands. Old-style figures, also called expert figures, are these 0123456789. Aligning figures are these 0123456789. Old-style figures are similar to uppercase and lowercase letters. They have ascenders and descenders. This allows the text to look uniform. A date set within the body copy 12/23/2012 will read as uppercase and lowercase letters. Alternatively, a date set with aligning characters, 12/23/2012, will look like a line of capital letters. Old-style figures also exist in italic form, and as with italic text, a slight size adjustment may be necessary. Some typefaces, such as Century Expanded, do not have accompanying old-style figures. This does not make them evil. This only indicates the designer, such as Morris Fuller Benton and Century Expanded, designed the font without them. **SA**

VIRGINIA 1607
VIRGINIA 1607

Thou shall use aligning figures with all caps

Yes

·······

Commentary When we read we look at individual characters, and reading becomes difficult when the characters are too similar. Imagine reading *War and Peace* typeset entirely in Helvetica. Reading is also interrupted when there is an abrupt change of shape. ALIGNING FIGURES, **0123456789**, MAINTAIN THE SAME SHAPE AS CAPITAL LETTERS. They do not have ascenders or descenders, and are uniform in height. Sans-serif fonts traditionally only have aligning figures. This was based on a rejection of classical forms, and a preference for

minimalism and simplicity. Recent typefaces, such as Alfa Sans, designed by Jens Gelhaar, include old-style figures. A common mistake is to use old-style figures with all capital letters as a headline. In the hopes of creating a design that is classic and traditional, a designer is tempted to use the seemingly more formal old-style figures. This creates a disjointed reading experience. Reading a line of all capital letters inexplicably switches to uppercase and lowercase characters. Do not be tempted by this affectation. It may look "fancy," but it is only incorrect. **SA**

Thou shall not use horizontal or vertical scaling to distort fonts

Commentary Don't be surprised if there's a gasp of horror and a shake of of the head any time someone asks if this is an acceptable means of treating type. As one of the most universally accepted "bad practices" in typography, it is still common among inexperienced graphic designers and typographers. Distorting the type in such a way plays havoc with the balance of the typeface's structure and creates unusual and awkward stroke widths in the characters. In short, it just looks awful! After the typeface designer and/or foundry have spent so much time and skill creating a beautifully weighted, consistent font family, stretching or squeezing it to "improve" it shows a serious lack of respect! If you do wish for a typeface with a wider character width, or a typeface that is compressed with a large cap height, then there are plenty of "extended" and "condensed" (sometimes called "compressed") typefaces available. **PD**

Thou shall not stroke your type so that it destroys the integrity of the letterforms

stroke

Commentary Look, everyone enjoys a little stroke now and again, but let's not get carried away. If the stroking becomes too heavy, you can barely recognize the form being smothered with such heavy attention. Innuendos aside, there are few times when stroking a typeface can be justified. (Production needs and trapping notwithstanding.) When a little fattening is absolutely necessary, it is important to truly consider what you're hoping to accomplish. If you're applying more than a point of stroke, there is a good chance that you're forcing the letterforms to do things they were never designed to do. Should you look closer, you will likely find that you have created some odd jags and such as well. If you really must have your type carrying such heft, perhaps I can interest you in a bolder font altogether. After all, what's the point in using a typeface, if it is no longer recognizable? **JF**

037

Thou shall not ruin a typeface with a filter effect

Commentary The computer allows us to stretch, squeeze, slant, and warp type. There are a multitude of filters that open the door for this abuse. You may argue that this activity is acceptable because filters exist to do this. Cars can be driven into trees, but that doesn't mean they should be. If you consider type as being made of the hardest substance in the universe, your life will be better. Type is not rubber. It is not soft clay. Claude Garamond did not spend decades drawing Garamond, only to have it inflated and distorted.

If you need a specific effect for a project, find a typeface that has the desired attributes. Rather than warping a typeface to create something taller, find a well-drawn condensed font. It is the mark of a poor designer to rely on filters and special effects. A good, solid idea will not require the Ocean Glass Ripple filter for the headline. Simple, clear, and beautifully crafted elements create good solutions. Adding filters and effects to create interest is comparable to pouring ketchup over a perfectly grilled steak. **SA**

Thou shall learn how to customize type successfully

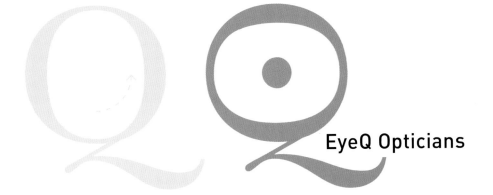

EyeQ Opticians

Commentary Not to be confused with a "custom typeface," which is a face designed from the ground up for a specific use or client, there are two situations where one might refer to type as customized. One situation would be where a designer has taken an existing letterform and redrawn it slightly by extending the serifs, by adding a swash, by removing part of a bowl, and so on. It's quite common for logo design specialists, for example, to customize a typeface in this way in order to set it apart from the original and to create a unique font for their client's identity. When this is done well, and when the concept behind the editing is supportive of the rationale for the changes, highly successful results can be achieved. The other situation would be to take an existing typeface and simply distort it in some way or add a filter effect, as described in Rule #37. But especially in this latter case, always try to honor the character of a typeface when you attempt any customization in order to retain the qualities conceived by the face's original designer. **TS**

Do not try this, it will never work

Thou shall not reverse 6pt text out of a black background

Commentary One of the goals of most clients is to create solutions that communicate. In order to communicate clearly, it is necessary to read copy. While small, delicate typography in white looks wonderful on the screen, most of us need to enlarge the view to 200 percent to read it. A computer screen is made of light. Light passes through the monitor onto our optical nerves. The result is a glowing and bright white on a solid black surface. Printed matter is different. Light bounces off the surface of a printed object. The white copy will never be as bright as a screen, and the black solid will never be as dense and consistent. Reversing small type sizes out of black does not work. It is easier to read black copy on a white background. In printed work, a solid black background requires heavy ink coverage. Smaller type will begin to "fill in" as the coverage is denser. The only available option will be to decrease ink coverage, resulting in a thin and light black. The solution is to maintain a size and weight that will not be adversely affected. **SA**

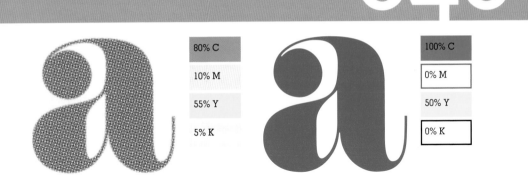

| 80% C |
| 10% M |
| 55% Y |
| 5% K |

| 100% C |
| 0% M |
| 50% Y |
| 0% K |

Thou shall specify at least one plate as 100% tint for colored type

Commentary One of the negative aspects of the digital age is the lack of understanding of the physical world. When designing on the computer, everything looks perfect. The colors are solid, the lines are precise. The type created with 58% cyan and 12% magenta looks like a nice blue. The printouts that are shown to the client look fine, and we explain that the colors may be slightly different when actually printed. Then tragedy strikes. On press, the type is soft and blurry. The printer adds more ink, and the problem is exacerbated. Hopefully, the type will become sharper when the press sheets dry. But they don't. Why did this happen? Because when the type is created with percentages of cyan and magenta, a halftone screen is created. Halftone screens are made up of tiny dots. Hence, the letterforms are made of tiny dots and will always be soft. The solution is to always use one process color at 100 percent value. One plate will be clean line art, with no halftone dots, and your type will therefore be sharp and refined. **SA**

041

Thou shall not use excessive leading in body copy

But we can perhaps remember—if only for a time—that those who live with us are our brothers, that they share with us the same short moment of life, that they seek—as do we—nothing but the chance to live out their lives in purpose and in happiness, winning what satisfaction and fulfillment that they can.

···

Commentary Let's begin with the basics. Leading is the space between lines of text. The name comes from the actual pieces of lead that were used by metal typesetters. Appropriate leading allows us to read clearly. Too little leading will make copy too dense and hard to read, as if someone were mumbling. Too much leading and the copy will be too open and hard to read. There will be too much space between the lines and it will read as if someone were speaking with long pauses in the middle of a sentence. At the end of each line, the reader will need to stop, go to the kitchen for a glass of water, then start the next line. Traditionally, type exists to be read. It is not meant to occupy space as a funny compositional element that serves no other purpose. Excessive leading may be "interesting" visually, but it is unreadable. And, in the end, making typography unreadable is passive aggressive behavior toward the reader. **SA**

Thou shall not use CAPS for long passages of body copy

WE'VE ALREADY DISCUSSED IN RULE #9 THE IMPORTANCE OF KEEPING THE TYPEFACE SIMPLE IN ORDER TO ENSURE THE LEGIBILITY OF LONG PASSAGES OF TEXT. HOWEVER, WITH EVEN JUST THE ONE TYPEFACE EMPLOYED, IT'S STILL EASY TO CREATE DIFFICULTIES FOR THE READER BY SETTING ALL THE TEXT IN CAPITAL LETTERS (OR UPPERCASE) THROUGHOUT. IT'S UNIVERSALLY RECOGNIZED (AND MUCH RESEARCH HAS BEEN DONE ON THE SUBJECT) THAT MIXED LOWERCASE AND UPPERCASE BLOCKS OF TEXT ARE EASIER TO READ THAN ALL UPPERCASE. THIS IS PRIMARILY DUE TO THE FACT THAT, DESPITE UPPERCASE TEXT APPEARING LARGER WHEN SET AT THE SAME SIZE, IT HAS NO ASCENDERS OR DESCENDERS. AS SUCH, THE LOWERCASE LETTERS HAVE MORE VARIATION IN THEIR APPEARANCE AND ARE THEREFORE EASIER TO RECOGNIZE, SPEEDING UP THE PROCESS OF READING. ANOTHER KEY POINT IS THAT USE OF UPPERCASE CAN COME ACROSS AS AGGRESSIVE AND SO GIVE THE IMPRESSION THAT THE AUTHOR IS SHOUTING AT YOU. EMPLOYING MIXED CASE FOR THE BULK OF THE TEXT CREATES A GENTLER, MORE MODERATE TONE AND HELPS GIVE THE OCCASIONAL USE OF CAPITALS GREATER IMPACT.

Commentary We've already discussed in Rule #9 the importance of keeping the typeface simple in order to ensure the legibility of long passages of text. However, with even just one typeface employed, it's still easy to create difficulties for the reader by setting all the text in uppercase. It's universally recognized (and much research has been done on the subject) that mixed lowercase and uppercase blocks of text are easier to read than all uppercase. This is primarily due to the fact that, despite uppercase text appearing larger when set at the same size, it has no ascenders or descenders. As such, the lowercase letters have more variation in their appearance and are therefore easier to recognize, speeding up the process of reading. Another key point is that use of uppercase can come across as aggressive and so give the impression that the author is shouting at you. Employing mixed case for the bulk of the text creates a gentler, more moderate tone and helps give the occasional use of capitals greater impact. **PD**

Thou shall not have excessive amounts of reversed-out text

This is too much reversed out text. This is too much reversed out text. This is too much reversed out text. This is too much reversed out text. This is too much reversed out text. This is too much reversed out text. This is too much reversed out text. This is too much reversed out text. This is too much reversed out text. This is too much reversed out text. This is too much reversed out text. This is too much reversed out text. This is too much reversed out text. This is too much reversed out text. This is too much reversed out text. This is too much reversed out text. This is too much reversed out text. This is too much reversed out text. This is too much reversed out text.

This is too much reversed out text. This is too much reversed out text. This is too much reversed out text. This is too much reversed out text. This is too much reversed out text. This is too much reversed out text. This is too much reversed out text. This is too much reversed out text. This is too much reversed out text. This is too much reversed

Commentary There are few truths as self-evident as the fact that black text on a white background is the easiest way for the eye to digest information and communicate it back to our brain. What we do with it after that is up to the individual, but the first part is true for most everyone. Thousands of years of writing, and no shortage of academic and scientific study, have borne this out. Given that the bulk of text is presented as such, for this very reason, reversing the course can have a huge impact. You still retain contrast, yet reversed-out text grabs your attention just by being different. It's like a feathered hat. Few people are wearing them, so everyone notices. But you know what will burn your retinas? A feathered skirt, blazer, and boots combo. That only works on Big Bird. The same is true for reversed-out text. Anything more than just a little is tough to enjoy. **JF**

THOU SHALL NOT OVER-STYLE HEADINGS

Commentary When designing a book, for instance, the purpose of the headings and sub-headings is not only to separate and order the text but also to aid navigation. Over the course of hundreds of pages, it is vital that the reader is able to find with ease the section or subsection they wish to read. It is therefore important that headings remain stylistically consistent throughout. It's tempting, with so many styling variables at our disposal, to start applying treatments to headers until we end up with a "dog's dinner" of typographical applications. Keep it simple and concentrate more on balancing the size of the headings with the size of the body text so that you get a clear hierarchy among the different heading levels, and a visual connection between those levels. Using a secondary typeface that differs from the body text is also fine, but remember to practice restraint at all times; by doing so, your designs will be cleaner and more professional. **PD**

Thou shall not add two spaces after a period

es. ·· Ab

Commentary Ever since the introduction of movable type, the correct amount of space following a period has been a source of debate. Type set by hand utilized variously sized "spacers" depending on the chosen font and it was down to the compositor to decide what looked right. The introduction of the typewriter in the late 19th century changed all this because the type was monospaced, meaning each letter was allocated the same character width. A single space after a period was deemed insufficient so the practice of double-spacing was taught widely, with hot-metal Linotype operators adopting the convention alongside regular typing-pool employees. Nowadays, modern digital fonts contain proportional kerning pairs and a slightly wider space is always added after a period, so a double space is no longer required. It's ultimately down to the typographer but the convention is, always add a single space after a period. **TS**

Thou shall apply an indent to the beginning of each new paragraph of body copy

Commentary Large amounts of body copy will typically be divided into paragraphs, which are made up of multiple sentences that ease the reading process and create pauses for the reader. When a new paragraph begins it will start on a new line, and there are rules regarding how this new paragraph should be presented. If there is no clear line break preceding the new paragraph, then the first line of the new paragraph should be indented to signify that a new paragraph starts. You should never indent and have a line break, as the two treatments are in effect a duplication of each other. You only need to signify it once. However, there are exemptions from indenting: never the first paragraph and never after a heading or subheading. **PD**

047

Thou shall not indent a paragraph that follows a heading or paragraph break

Commentary As Rule #46 has explained, when setting large amounts of body copy, it will be structured as paragraphs; a styling has to be applied to create paragraphs that signify pauses for the reader. It may be that you decide to have line breaks between each paragraph so that they are clearly separated. This approach would probably be used more in literature or promotional print items rather than other types of publishing such as newspapers because, in the latter, space is at a premium. Be aware that this approach breaks up the flow when reading and is a bit too "stop–start." If you are employing line breaks, you should never indent—the two treatments basically fulfill the same function. Likewise, if a heading precedes the start of a new paragraph, there is no need to indent. **PD**

Thou shall not indent a paragraph that starts at the top of a column or page (unless house style say otherwise)

Commentary The rules governing the indentation of paragraphs are invariably linked to either a publisher's house style or style rules in corporate guidelines, so a degree of flexibility is important. That said, it is essential to be consistent when setting the text, particularly where a new paragraph begins at the top of a column or page. In the books I have designed, body text is indented when a new paragraph begins at the top of a column or page. In corporate literature, however, I find that, because the page grid will often have more columns of text per page, it's cleaner not to indent at the top of a column. Discuss with the client whether there are any house styles before you begin, as the decision may have already been made for you. **PD**

Thou shall set the first few words of a sentence following a drop cap in small caps

HERE IS an ex of what I hav planning to s in regards to using r following a drop cap. you to ease into thin

Commentary Think of this in the same way you might a foyer in a house, or better yet, a hallway or atrium before you are to enter into a huge performance space. The heart of the space still lies ahead, where you will spend hours digesting a barrage of information, unless it is a night at the opera, where you might just catch up on some sleep, but that is another book altogether. Outside the arena, there are blaring and bold signs welcoming

you in. Those are the drop caps in our typographic world. Once we are nestled in our row, that is the body copy getting ready to take the stage—the meat of the evening. What is needed is a visual transition from the huge drop cap to the workmanlike body copy. Enter the sensible small cap to walk us to our seat. **JF**

Thou shall not use tabs to create indents

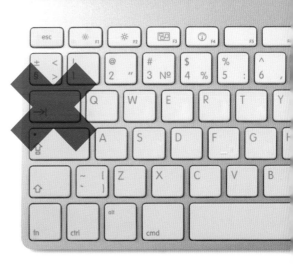

Commentary Tabs exist to position text at specific measurements within a line length. They are useful when creating tables of information. Tabs should not be used to create indents. Indents move the text inward from the left or right edge of the line length. Indents should be used, oddly, to create indents. The first line indent of a paragraph can be set, and then each subsequent paragraph will follow the same measurement. If a tab is used to do this, the designer will need to manually insert a tab space. When multiple paragraphs need indents, this manual approach may lead to errors. A tab might be forgotten. The tab measurement may be set incorrectly. If there are copy revisions, and there always are copy revisions, a manually set tab may move and end up in the middle of a line. A first line indent is the correct approach. This will not affect any copy changes, and the manual input of individual tabs is not necessary. **SA**

051

Thou shall hang lines of text from a tab in a bulleted list

1. When a bulleted or numbered list contains items that run to more than one line, it is common to "hang" the text from the bullet or number.

2. A paragraph may also be hung from the first line of text -- often with a run-in head of bold or italic when no bullet or number is present. In either case, the hanging indent more clearly marks the item in the list.

3. When a bulleted or numbered list contains items that run to more than one line, it is common to "hang" the text from the bullet or number.

4. A paragraph may also be hung from the first line of text --often with a run-in head of bold or italic

Commentary A solid swath of body copy is like a team: to be successful it needs everyone to fully understand and perform their role. When someone starts to freelance and do their own thing, it weakens the whole operation. Each piece has a job, with specific functions, and with good reason. When you have a bulleted list, one must understand each role completely, then all of the decisions that follow are easy. You have a title or main head that deserves some attention on its own.

This means that it starts on the left to grab your eye immediately. You might have some intro copy. Not as important, but still needs your attention, so it starts on the left. Then you have the tabbed copy, indented to show that it is a subsection. The copy with each tab is a self-sufficient little burst and belongs together as a single notion. So why would you let it slip over to the left on the next line? It's not a header or body copy. It's a tab and proud of it. **JF**

Thou shall learn the difference between a typeface and a font

OTF

8opt

Commentary Designers regularly refer to typefaces and fonts as the same thing but there's an important, albeit subtle, terminological difference. A typeface is a set of characters that is independent of an individual point size but shares other characteristics such as the width of its strokes, the style of its serifs, indeed whether it is serif or a sans serif, and so on. Given this, you can say that Archer Bold (used for the large numbers at the top of each page in this book) is a *typeface*.

A font on the other hand is all the characters, including numerals, punctuation, glyphs, and so on, for a typeface at one specific point size. Therefore, 80pt Archer Bold is a *font*. It's a simple distinction but one worth knowing, especially if you have a tendency toward type-geekiness. One likes to be completist about these things, after all! TS

Thou shall not confuse x-height with cap height

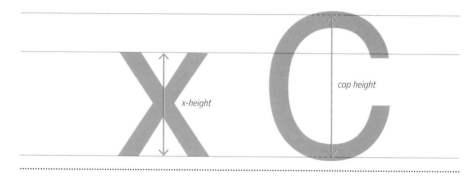

x-height

cap height

Commentary It's a very important rule to remember and, once learned, the definitions of each will stay with you forever. To clarify, the x-height of a typeface starts from the baseline, on which all the characters sit, and reaches up to the height of the lowercase letters (not including their ascenders and descenders). To see how differing typefaces have a range of x-heights, create a line of type, duplicate it, change the font, overlay it, and examine the differences. The ascenders and descenders on letters with small x-heights will look more pronounced. Larger x-heights will make the text look heavier and more solid, so an increase in the leading may be required to compensate. The cap height simply refers to the height of the capital letters from the baseline to the top. Be aware that rounded uppercase letters sit above the cap height and below the baseline, so this measurement doesn't apply to them. Their additional size is called an "overshoot." **PD**

Thou shall consider a font's x-height when specifying line feed

Everything on this line is 28pt

Commentary When I select which typeface I'm going to use for a new project, I like to start by setting blocks of 9pt body text with 12pt line feed (or leading) to see how my various choices look. The $^{9}/_{12}$pt setting isn't an arbitrary choice, but rather a rough average of the values one might choose for the point size and leading of body text. One of the first things I tend to note is the variation in the x-height between my font choices, partly because the x-height contributes largely to the feel of the setting but also because it influences the leading required for comfortable line-by-line scanning. A font with a large x-height (such as Helvetica) will likely need a little more leading (or a reduction in point size) than a smaller x-height (such as Centaur) would require, and this needs to be taken into account when planning your layout and grid. You should also take the height and depth of the ascenders and descenders into account when specifying line feed. **TS**

055

Thou shall learn what "leading" means and what it does

Leading is named as such based on the strips of lead that old typesetters used to separate lines of metal type. In essence, it is the distance from the baseline of one line of type laid out to another. You may also hear it referred to as line spacing in conversation.

Commentary "Leading" has a name derived from the olden times of typesetting, yet it is one of the most important things to understand in becoming a competent designer. You may also hear this called "line feed," but that is usually from people that don't fully grasp leading. The term comes from the strips of lead that typesetters would use to create specific space between lines of metal type. The way it is applied in the modern era is much more varied and powerful. Based on a premise of using 120 percent of the size of the type being displayed, the default setting for most programs works fairly well. But this is an area where the designer can instantly create a response from the viewer interacting with his or her layout (feeling tense and claustrophobic as I tighten the paragraph leading, or airy and loose as I increase it?) and should be fully explored and understood. **JF**

Consistent leading within a paragraph is extremely important. Changing this can create an unplanned effect on the reader as they are made uncomfortable. One has to consider that the paragraph is intended to contain a single thought and should therefore be kept cohesive.

Thou shall keep consistent leading within a paragraph

Commentary Now that we know how powerful leading is, and it is incredibly powerful, we have to understand why we can't abuse it. If you walk down a corridor and it slowly gets narrower, you feel pretty uncomfortable by the end, and certainly you are having a different experience than when you started out just a few feet back. A corridor that opens wide by the end gives the reverse effect, but it is just as jarring. The same is true if you jockey around with the leading in a paragraph. By nature, a paragraph is a complete thought and should be kept cohesive. The viewer has to have the same interpretation at the beginning as they do at the end. No matter what the desired effect is, the point is to remain consistent in order to achieve it. **JF**

057

Thou shall understand paragraph spacing and use it wisely

In speaking about paragraph spacing, one should take into account a number of factors, such as how the information is to be received and digested. How much space is available on the page? Should the designer be creative with an option? Or is it best to go with a tried and true solution like the following half line?

In speaking about paragraph spacing, one should take into account a number of factors, such as how the information is to be received and digested. How much space is available on the page? Should the designer be creative with an option? Or is it best to go with a tried and true solution like the following half line?

Commentary Paragraphs are formed so that we can digest the information in reasonable blocks. This is a simple idea, but one that few designers seem to take into account. With that perspective, the space between paragraphs takes on a heightened importance. There are a number of ways to accomplish getting our eye to acknowledge that we have finished one paragraph and are starting another, and each one has its benefits and deterrents. The trick is in finding the best solution for your particular project—indents (or for the true wild child, outdents) are not as visually clean as a line break with a half-line space, but they do conserve space. Typographers of the past used various creative ways to make this happen, rarely with readable results, but the masters could finesse it at times (for example, symbols marking the space between paragraphs as the body copy continues to run and run and run—a magazine sidebar mainstay.) If you understand the process, the answers become more evident. **JF**

Thou shall not apply excessive tracking to body copy

Commentary The terms tracking and kerning quite often get confused. Kerning is the adjustment of space between individual letter pairs, whereas tracking is the adjustment of letter spacing of entire lines or paragraphs of text. Tracking is a useful feature when setting body text but it must be used sparingly so as not to cause problems with legibility. Too much negative tracking and a sentence or paragraph will appear dense compared to the rest of the text. Too much positive tracking and the text will look too airy, blurring the distinction between letters and words and making it difficult to read. The benefits of tracking are that you can apply it to entire paragraphs, to single lines, or to a single word, and this can enable you to pull back widows and orphans and tidy up awkward line breaks. As a rule of thumb, when using a software package like Adobe InDesign, I would never go past +/–25 as a maximum. **PD**

Thou shall always kern unsightly character combinations

Commentary Quite often, although the typeface you have chosen may be working well, the spacing between some of the letters can look uneven. This is a very common aspect of typography that designers deal with on a day-to-day basis; to compensate, you need to kern the letters. When setting uppercase text, the issues are more evident, as is the case with letters such as T, V, and W, which force the following letter to sit some distance away. When creating their fonts, typeface designers do consider many of the letters that sit awkwardly together (for example, Kn, To, Ve, Wi) and create "kerning pairs" to eliminate the spacing issues. More often than not, however, it's up to you to adjust and eliminate the unsightly spacing. To do so, simply decrease (or increase) the kerning between the characters so that they are better balanced and appear evenly spaced in relation to the rest of the word. **PD**

Thou shall always kern headlines manually

Commentary The familiar adage, "The bigger they are, the harder they fall," can be applied to type too. Design software and kerning pairs work in tandem to control the character spacing of all type and at point sizes below 14pt it's hardly ever necessary to apply any manual kerning. It's a good job too—imagine the amount of work needed to sort that lot out. However, as point sizes increase for crossheads and headlines, the character spacing becomes more visible and some attention is often required. Problem pairs can involve, but aren't limited to, any characters that don't have vertical stems at the side, so A, K, T, V, W, and Y are common culprits. In reality, any number of character pairs in both uppercase and lowercase may need some manual kerning—it depends on the typeface. When you're searching for kerning problems, try squinting at the setting as it helps to make the awkward white spaces between characters more evident. **TS**

Thou shall not use negative letter spacing

NEGATIVE

Commentary If you've ever been sitting on a train or bus and had more butts than can possibly fit on the bench with you try to squeeze on anyway (no time to hit the gym this week, Jim? Those sure are a lot of bags you've got, Mary...) then you know what we are on about with negative letter spacing. This doesn't mean that you can't nuzzle together to get the job done on occasion—some tracking work to pull up an orphan here and there can be required. What we are talking about is the pulling together of letterforms to the point that they are uncomfortable or right on top of one another. They just weren't designed to work that way, much in the same manner that too many people sitting in our lap leaves us suffocating to the point of needing the bus to pull over at the hospital rather than our desired stop. **JF**

Thou shall not exceed a character count of 80 per line in a measure

LINE
LIMIT
80

Commentary For the sake of readability, the designer should ensure that the measure (or line length) isn't too long. Very long lines can mean that the reader loses their place mid-sentence or when shifting their eyes to the start of the following line—a frustrating experience if you have a whole book ahead of you! A way of getting around this is to check the character count in an individual line. A generally accepted standard is around 45–75 characters per line; at a push you can go to 80, but this depends on the typeface chosen. On the flip side, a very short measure means that the reader's eyes will be continually zipping back and forth, ensuring a disagreeable reading experience. Working within or close to the limits will help to improve your design. **PD**

063

Thou shall set the second line of a paragraph longer than the first

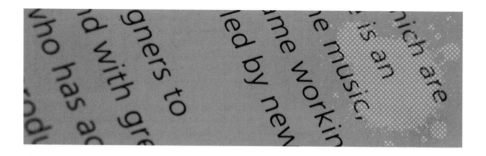

Commentary Once we start walking, we definitely appreciate some forward progress. Any step that has to be retraced, even if it's a half-step pause, is wasted motion. When we read, it's the same quality that takes over, and once we get going, it's hard to stop us on our stroll toward comprehension. That is why we like to have the second line of a paragraph set longer than the first. The indented white space, if it is shorter, gives us pause. Creating this is a combination of selective line breaks and tracking as needed. Ragging our copy is an art form in its own right. It is important to note that this should not take precedence over other hard rules of typography (don't end the second line with a dangling "a" or "it" or track out +60 just to make it happen) but it should be attempted wherever possible. **JF**

Thou shall set the penultimate line of a paragraph longer than the last

Commentary As we have already discussed, the paragraph is a construct of writers; it doesn't actually occur naturally like a sentence (which is a full thought as if uttered in conversation). Paragraphs are there so that we can digest information in easy stages. Thus, we have come up with numerous tools to let the reader know exactly when a paragraph is ending, and another one is starting. In order for these to work, one of the most important aspects is that the last line of set type will be shorter than the line before it, creating a bit of white space to alert the eye to the change. A simple meal is structured in much the same way: appetizer (slightly shorter first line), entrée (slightly longer second line, going into the body, or main portion, of the paragraph), and the dessert (shorter final line.) If the dessert is larger than the entrée, you have no idea what kind of meal you have eaten and if it is over. **JF**

065

Thou shall not allow a line to break on the words "it" or "is"

Commentary This is one of those rules that really showcases those that are the true masters of paragraph ragging. You won't find it in any manual, or stated as a hard rule in a textbook, but if you work with savvy folks that have been in the trenches of publication design, this is often one of the first tips that they pass on. When working out justified type, it is harder to accomplish, but when you have flush left or right, you should be willing to rework a paragraph seven different ways to make it happen. Why do we care so much? Because finishing a line as such leaves a massive hanging thought and causes an awkward pause in our comprehension. The easiest practice is simply to read the text aloud. Once you do that, you will never let a line end in "it" or "is" again. We would never talk that way; why should we force ourselves to read that way? **JF**

Thou shall not hyphenate words of less than seven characters

Commentary Many designers are happy to hyphenate short words, but for me the minimum acceptable number of characters a word should contain before it can be hyphenated is seven. This in turn means a minimum of four characters before a hyphen and no fewer than three characters following a hyphenated line break. Fortunately, these parameters can be set within a paragraph style sheet at the beginning of a project to ensure the consistency of all body copy (see Rule #69). Why seven? It's partly a visual thing, as I don't believe two characters followed by a hyphen looks great, but it's also an editorial consideration, as personally I don't think words of five characters or less read cleanly when they're hyphenated. Experienced readers store words as "shapes" to speed up the reading process and seeing the first few characters of a word helps us to fill in the rest before we've scanned to the start of the next line. If you only have one or two characters to work with, this process doesn't happen. **TS**

Yes

Thou shall not mix centered and flush-left or -right text

....

Commentary For hundreds of years, typographic layouts used a largely symmetrical, centered approach. Headlines, subheads, and body text were centered or justified. Symmetrical typography was a product of available technology and the printing press. In the 1920s, Jan Tschichold championed a new approach. His frustration with complex, illegible Victorian and Gothic German forms led him to a system of sans-serif fonts, more negative space, and asymmetric typography. He considered asymmetry to be more legible, vibrant, and powerful.

This does not mean that centered typography inherently wrong. It is entirely appropriate in certain contexts. Mixing centered and flush-left or -right text, however, is wrong. It is similar to mixing a simple white t-shirt with red velvet pantaloons. It's not pretty, and looks foolish. As with most things in life, maintaining consistency creates clarity. A consistent centered layout tells the viewer how and where to look for information. The same is true for an asymmetric layout. Mixing the two creates confusion and chaos. **SA**

Thou shall not use justified text over a short measure

Commentary If a designer can spend several years obsessively refining the word spacing and kerning of a justified paragraph, then justifying a short line length is okay. For those with less than a decade, this is a bad idea. Justified type requires a minimum number of characters to be acceptable. This is about mathematics. Too few characters, and the word spacing will become enormous to create a justified axis. Large word spacing will create "rivers" of negative space within a paragraph and thus make reading more difficult. Good typography should be invisible.

It facilitates reading and enhances understanding. Creating a justified line length that feels effortless is the correct solution. Typography stops being invisible when we are faced with a discrepancy, such as large word spaces. When justifying text, a good rule of thumb with line length measures is to use no more than 80 characters (approximately three alphabets), and no fewer than 26 characters (one alphabet). But the best approach is to set the text with a line measure that has an optically consistent amount of word and letter space. **SA**

069

Thou shall check justification settings for justified text

Justification	Minimum	Desired	Maximum	
Word Spacing:	85%	100%	125%	OK
Letter Spacing:	0%	0%	0%	Cancel
Glyph Scaling:	100%	100%	100%	☑ Preview

Auto Leading: 150%

Single Word Justification: Align Left ⬍

Composer: Adobe Single-line Composer ⬍

Commentary Desktop publishing (DTP) programs InDesign® and QuarkXPress® both provide the means to apply manual settings for justification. The settings are only applicable to justified text, as ragged text uses the optimum letter and word spacing built into a font. If you opt for justified alignment and the word spacing at your chosen font size looks too gappy, or too tight, the justification settings will help fix things. A value of 100% for word spacing or 0% for letter spacing is equal to "no manual adjustment" in real terms. If you want to close up space, enter a value less than 100% for word spacing or -0% for letter spacing; opening up space requires a value greater than 100% for words or +0% for letters; and so on. Play around with a paragraph of dummy copy to see how different values reflow the text—it's the best way to learn how the functionality works. My tip would be to concentrate on the minimum and maximum word spacing, leaving the desired setting at the optimum 100%, and always leave the letter spacing set to 0%. **TS**

different and unfamiliar (but delicious!) cuts of meat to the British public; a brother and sister determined to create the perfect chocolate and a car park full of chilli enthusiasts battling to make the best bowl of red. You'll come across scientists who are saving the Scottish fishing industry and historians who cook to unlock the past, have Sunday dinner (on a Thursday) with a French chef in his village gourmand, and hunker down with a very patriotic chicken. Many of these people have spent decades pursuing their own ideals of perfection, and the results are truly inspiring. This book's title is, in part, an acknowledgement of that, and a tribute to them.

Perfection is, of course, an incredibly subjective thing. Even the seemingly simple task of choosing which dishes to include in the series turned out to be a nightmare, and I knew I was bound to upset many people by leaving out their particular favourite. 'Where's steak and kidney pie, toad in the hole, bread and butter pudding? Where's prawn cocktail?' I could imagine people saying. Nonetheless, after holing up in a meeting room and vowing not to emerge until we had thrashed out a viable running order, the BBC team and I eventually had a list that seemed to have something for everyone – a range of undeniably popular meals that also offered lots of interesting challenges in the kitchen. Sixteen dishes that people could really get their teeth into.

Even so, there was heated discussion among us. Roast beef or roast chicken? Italian or American pizza? Trifle or tiramisu? There were fierce advocates of all points of view. It reinforced my opinion that, ultimately, there's no such thing as perfection. What's perfect for one is not going to be perfect for all – one man's meat really is another man's poison. Each of us has our own idea of what constitutes perfection, drawing heavily on a potent and highly personalised mix of emotions, memories and surroundings. Despite the book's title, I knew from the outset that I wouldn't be claiming my recipes were in any way 'definitive'. But I reckoned that, by using my technical skill and scientific knowledge, by talking to producers and artisans and chefs and their custo-

8 . TOTAL PERFECTION

mers, I could pin down some of the things that made these dishes work.

While the dictionary defines 'perfection' as 'the state of being perfect', it also offers a second definition that is equally important to this book: honing a recipe through continual experimentation. Trying out ideas and then revising and retrying them until you've got something special, unique. The TV series gave me the opportunity to get out and try my hand at all sorts of things I'd never encountered before, and I was as excited about this as I was about the chance to explore memory and nostalgia in food because that's how I started in the restaurant business.

Although I've had help and advice from many people, I'm a self-taught chef. My passion for cooking began at sixteen when my parents took me and my sister L'Oustau de Baumanière, a Michelin three-star restaurant. None of us had ever been anywhere like that before, and I was totally knocked out by it – not just the fabulous food but the whole multisensory experience: the sound of fountains and cicadas, the heady smell of lavender, the sight of the waiters carving lamb at the table or pouring lobster sauce into soufflés.

I knew at once that I wanted to be part of it.

For the next ten years – like a car enthusiast dedicatedly stripping down and reassembling a vintage TR7 or Morris Minor – I took apart and examined every aspect of classic French cuisine, trying to perfect the kind of experience I had had in France. As the results of my cooking got better and my confidence grew, I began to explore how I might create dishes that matched up to my own ideals of perfection – meat in which the robust, earthy, browned surface gave way to a gratifyingly soft and velvety inner texture, for example, or a parsley mousse whose silky airiness seemed too fragile to contain any strong taste, so that when it melted in your mouth the depth of flavour came as a distinct and pleasurable surprise. And, mindful of how much the power of the Oustau experience lay in its appeal not just to my tastebuds but to all of my senses, I sought to capture that multisensory effect in

INTRODUCTION . 9

Thou shall avoid creating "rivers" in justified text

Commentary When a text is justified, a distracting visual oddity can often occur whereby the spaces between words arrange themselves on top of one another, forming a curving white line running vertically through the paragraph—something referred to as a "river." This can appear in flush-left, -right, and centered type but, because of the way justified type increases the word spacing by forcing the line of type to the full measure, the chance of rivers occurring increases. Rectifying the problem is straightforward. The first step is to introduce hyphenation into the setting; this can be done manually if you wish to reduce the number of hyphens that appear, or it can be set up automatically in your DTP software. Alternatively, you can track some of the affected lines in or out to compensate. Problem solved! **PD**

Type and Typography   83

Thou shall not allow "widows" to appear in text

Commentary One of typography's more unusual terms, I've seen this occur so many times that even some of the most beautifully crafted work, on closer examination, has been marred by the oversight of not attending to widows. As opposed to orphans, they are single words or lines of text that have been separated from the rest of the paragraph and are either sitting at the top of the following column, or pushed over to the opposite page. There they sit all on their own, away from the rest of their text, creating an unsightly visual anomaly at the top of the column or page. To rectify and "save" the widow, review the column or page from where it has been forced over and track back these lines, which are more open (if justified) or are shorter (if flush-left), to pull back words and thereby eliminate the widow. The end result will be that the bottom of the column or page finishes cleanly with the end of a paragraph and the next page starts with a new one. **PD**

Thou shall not allow "orphans" to appear in text

Commentary An orphan (which, in my view, is commonly and mistakenly referred to as a *widow*—see Rule #71 for a definition) can be described as a single word sitting on its own at the end of a paragraph, or it can be the first line of a paragraph on its own at the bottom of a column or page. Visually, it is not very nice to look at and it hinders the flow of reading. In order to rectify this, either put in some soft returns in the text before it, pushing words over onto the next line and adding to the single word or, if there is space, track back certain lines to pull back words and pull the orphan back up to the preceding line. The same goes for the single line at the bottom of the column or page, although I would take the view that it is better to push it over than take it back so that the paragraphs have clean breaks between columns or pages. Better still, if you are working directly with an editor, ask them if the text can be edited in order to fix the problem. **PD**

073

Thou shall check that text is not formatted with "justify all lines" s e l e c t e d

Commentary There are three ways to set justified text, each of which treats the final line of a paragraph differently. The usual method is designated "justify with last line aligned left." This means any text on the final line of a paragraph will effectively not be justified at all—it will be ragged left. The character and word spacing probably won't match that of the lines that appear before it, but that is of course the nature of justified setting, and the reason that creating a pleasing result with justified text is often difficult to achieve. The second option is "justify with last line centered" which is never really going to work with running copy. The third option is "justify all lines" where the final line of a paragraph is set to the full measure regardless of how many words or characters it contains. If a line of copy almost fills a measure, falling short by only an em or so, this option will work perfectly well. Under any other circumstances it is best to avoid the option altogether, so never choose it as a default setting when buliding style sheets. **TS**

Thou shall not hyphenate text that is ragged right

Commentary I have had many a debate on this and, yes, I should "get out more," but I (and many others) see no reason for hyphenation when the body text is ragged right. Yes, line endings should certainly be tidied up, short words taken over, and orphans and widows dealt with. But the natural line breaks that appear with flush-left/ragged-right text negate the need to apply hyphenation. It is an additional element that, when added, actually hinders the reading process and doesn't look very good. **PD**

Thou shall not be scared of our useful little friend the hyphen

Commentary I'm not entirely sure why this is the case, but something is going on which has set designers against hyphenating at the end of lines. I'm going to make a bit of a distinction here as you see hyphens used to good (and often atrociously bad, I grant you) effect in newspapers and magazines all the time, but for some reason books, corporate brochures, and packaging featuring justified text seem to have become hyphen "no-go areas." The flip side of this is that the same books, brochures, and packs have simultaneously become safe havens for bad word spacing, which really does defeat the object entirely. The answer is, if you're really that scared of using hyphens, don't justify text, set it ragged. On the subject of ragged text, there's nothing to stop you hyphenating that either if you're having to deal with short measures and long words. Hang on a minute, the wail of dissent is getting louder and louder. I think I may have taken this argument a bit too far! **TS**

Thou shall use web-safe fonts for HTML text

```
<p>
<font face="Bookman Old
Style">Most of you will know
which fonts are...</font>
</p>
```

Commentary Most of you will know which fonts are web-safe so I'll pass on providing a list of them all here. I've always found the term a bit misleading as it implies that no other fonts will work online. What it really means is that web-safe fonts will appear as you intended them to on the largest number of PCs and Macs because they're installed by default as part of Windows or OS X. To be honest, and despite big improvements in the technology, it's still good advice to limit HTML text to the narrow choice of Arial, Georgia, Verdana, and so on because it's proven that they read well on screen. It's easy enough to use other fonts within a site if they're added as a graphic item, and online font hosting services mean that web-safe fonts are likely to become a thing of the past before too long. However, for big commercial sites with a large and diverse user-base, stick with web-safe fonts for the time being. **TS**

077

Thou shall <u>not</u> underline text for *emphasis*

Commentary Using an underline, or an underscore, to emphasize a word isn't a total no-no but there's a much better way—use italics. The term underscore derives from the name of the individual character which typists would apply to words by back-spacing and retyping an underline, and underscoring for emphasis is a bit of a "typing" thing rather than proper typesetting practice. Italics, particularly when used in running text, present a much more elegant solution and provide the required emphasis without interrupting the flow. This means emphasis is achieved "invisibly" without jolting the reader's attention away from the fluid run of the narrative. If you're designing an application form or diagram, for example, the rule doesn't apply so much—it's more appropriate for larger blocks of body copy. There's now another good reason for not using underscores, as online they denote a hyperlink, so any text that will be repurposed from a print project ideally shouldn't contain any underscores at all. **TS**

Thou shall use true typographer's quotation marks

Commentary These are sometimes called "smart quotes," which to me seems a bit over the top, as there aren't any other kinds of quotes you can use correctly. Whenever you need to highlight a quotation or utilize an apostrophe, please use the proper quotation marks that look like miniature floating pairs of sixes and nines. The marks that don't have any curly bits are called primes, or double primes if there are two of them together, and they specifically denote feet (double primes), inches, or seconds, so this isn't just a styling issue. The sixes open a quotation, the nines close a quotation and double-up as apostrophes, providing added value at no extra cost. Except to my dental bills that is, as seeing primes used incorrectly in the place of quotation marks makes me grind my teeth, so spare a thought. **TS**

Thou shall use correct accent marks

á é í ó ú ñ ü

á é í ó ú ñ ü

á é í ó ú ñ ü

á é í ó ú ñ ü

Commentary Despite our general assertion and expectation, the rest of the world doesn't do everything in English. They even have the nerve to add little squiggles, dashes, and dots over some of our precious letterforms. How dare they! It seems like some of these have a basis in how these people talk, you know, with those funny sounds that come out where we would have plainly said an "o" or an "e." It might seem humorous until you realize that we could use the same system just to help northerners and southerners understand each other. The reason we have printed matter at all is as a substitute to a person actually being there to say it in front of us. If they would have stood there pronouncing words as they occur in their natural environment, then we should respect those sounds. If this means mastering some of the keyboard shortcuts and special characters, well, we are learning something and broadening our horizons and showing respect on every level. **JF**

Thou shall use correctly formatted fractions

¼ ½ ¾ ¼ ½ ¾ ¼ ½ ¾ ¼ ½ ¾ ¼ ½ ¾ ¼ ½ ¾ ¼ ½ ¾ ¼ ½ ¾ ¼ ½ ¾ ¼ ½ ¾
¼ ½ ¾ ¼ ½ ¾ ¼ ½ ¾ ¼ ½ ¾ ¼ ½ ¾ ¼ ½ ¾ ¼ ½ ¾ ¼ ½ ¾ ¼ ½ ¾ ¼ ½ ¾
¼ ½ ¾ ¼ ½ ¾ ¼ ½ ¾ ¼ ½ ¾ ¼ ½ ¾ ¼ ½ ¾ ¼ ½ ¾ ¼ ½ ¾ ¼ ½ ¾ ¼ ½ ¾
¼ ½ ¾ ¼ ½ ¾ ¼ ½ ¾ ¼ ½ ¾ ¼ ½ ¾ ¼ ½ ¾ ¼ ½ ¾ ¼ ½ ¾ ¼ ½ ¾ ¼ ½ ¾
¼ ½ ¾ ¼ ½ ¾ ¼ ½ ¾ ¼ ½ ¾ ¼ ½ ¾ ¼ ½ ¾ ¼ ½ ¾ ¼ ½ ¾ ¼ ½ ¾ ¼ ½ ¾
¼ ½ ¾ ¼ ½ ¾ ¼ ½ ¾ ¼ ½ ¾ ¼ ½ ¾ ¼ ½ ¾ ¼ ½ ¾ ¼ ½ ¾ ¼ ½ ¾ ¼ ½ ¾
¼ ½ ¾ ¼ ½ ¾ ¼ ½ ¾ ¼ ½ ¾ ¼ ½ ¾ ¼ ½ ¾ ¼ ½ ¾ ¼ ½ ¾ ¼ ½ ¾ ¼ ½ ¾
¼ ½ ¾ ¼ ½ ¾ ¼ ½ ¾ ¼ ½ ¾ ¼ ½ ¾ ¼ ½ ¾ ¼ ½ ¾ ¼ ½ ¾ ¼ ½ ¾ ¼ ½ ¾

Commentary If you have the advantage of reading the copy before beginning a layout project, especially if you expect to be dealing with financials, or some form of numerical breakdown, I strongly advise that you start with typefaces that have full families and might even have specific versions for fractions. Regardless, this is a place where taking a shortcut makes for a very awkward piece of typesetting. There are few things as clunky as two numbers separated by a slash, when a proper, tight fraction is available. Think about it in the sense that a fraction should take up the equivalent visual space than a letter, thus less than if it were full rounded numbers, and you get the idea pretty quickly. Like the proper use of small caps, this is an area where the reader can instantly see the work of an experienced designer and appreciate a more sophisticated ability to deal with type. **JF**

081

1969–2011

Thou shall use an en-dash to indicate a range of values

....

Commentary The use, or misuse, of en-dashes is a common problem in the written content that we are sent. An en-dash should be used when numbers or words that denote a range need to be linked together or to signify an open range. For example, 1939–1945 and 100–200 BCE are examples of the en-dash being used in a closed range. Note that there is no space either side of the

en-dash. When typesetting these figures, and if one is using nonaligning numerals, it is worthwhile kerning a little space between the figures and the en-dash so that they don't look as though they are colliding. An open-ended range would be set as "2011–"; for words that are communicating a range it would look like this "January–December 2011." **PD**

text cat
es—bu
foreve

Thou shall use an em-dash to indicate a conversational break

Commentary Although used as often as its cousin, the en-dash, the em-dash is the correct punctuation mark to insert into a sentence when a conversational break is required. The em-dash, being more significant in presence than a comma, does provide greater emphasis in setting apart an aside in a sentence. At the same time, it is not as definite as a period, so the subject and intent of the sentence is carried through. For example, "Despite the disapproval of his friends—they thought he had forsaken his values—

Peter decided to use Comic Sans." In addition, it can be used to signify an emotive interruption into a sentence; for example, "I can't believe it's—," which works better than a period and signifies the speaker is left hanging. Its use seems to be decreasing, which I think is a shame. That said, be careful not to overuse the em-dash; it can be somewhat overpowering. Everything in moderation. **PD**

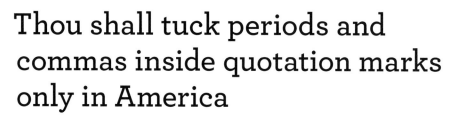

083

Thou shall tuck periods and commas inside quotation marks only in America

"Only in America."

Commentary No one is quite sure when it happened (maybe it was linked to that little "independence" dust up), but once British conventions were sent across the Atlantic, a few of them seemed to have fallen overboard, leaving the Yanks to make their own decisions. While Americans have removed the "u" in "colors" to reflect their pronunciation, other decisions are more closely linked to modern typesetting. The placement of punctuation in regards to quotation marks was formed in an earlier time, founded on the basic needs—namely that punctuation signaled the end of a sentence. So, of course it fell outside of the quotation mark, as that was part of the thought being expressed. However, American typesetters noted the awkward space it creates and, as one of many adjustments, experimented with it on the inside, thus creating a tighter space. This was soon adopted as the correct way to position of periods and commas. **JF**

Thou shall place periods and commas outside of quotation marks everywhere but America

"Outside of America".

Commentary While American typesetters would surely tell you that they have reengineered the fuddy duddy old-world ways to better effect (and in this case, it is hard to argue against the more appealing visual white space left by tucking the punctuation inside the quotation marks), that doesn't necessarily mean that we can expect that thousands of years of the written word will instantly abide by their new rules. Placing the periods and commas is based upon the intended use of the marks, to signal the end of a thought in conversation. Holding fast to that thinking, the periods and commas have to come after all other elements of that segment, and that has been the case in written text from the very beginning until now. While figuring out the differences in spelling certain words can occupy a lot of your time when trying to make a layout for a main audience in one country or another, this is the hardest practice to toggle back and forth on. **JF**

Thou shall hang quotation marks outside the paragraph margins

Commentary In order to achieve a smoothly aligned left edge for a pull quote or the body text, it's best to "hang" the quotation marks. This involves repositioning the opening quotation mark out to the left so that the initial letter of the text sits aligned with the rest. It's a simple task to do; if you are using a software package such as InDesign® for your layout, there's a feature under an option called "Story" where a palette window will contain a checkbox called "Optical Margin Alignment." Here you can key in the point size of the text you are using and it will refine the alignment and hang the punctuation for you. However, I always find that it is never quite enough to key in the exact match of the text size you have styled, so I always key in a size 20–30 percent bigger to ensure a crisper alignment. **PD**

grapr

Thou shall add a period after an ellipsis at the end of a sentence

n. . . . .

Commentary When an ellipsis is employed within the text it can be used in a number of ways. Dramatically, to create a pause in speech in the middle of a sentence (appearing with a space either side of the ellipsis). Or at the end of a sentence (preceded by a space), almost as if the writer has faded away, lost in thought. However, a common mistake is to leave the ellipsis at the end of a sentence unfinished.

I understand there to have been great debate about this in the past, so whether this entry adds fuel to the fire, who knows? In my professional opinion, however, it needs the period in order to provide closure to the sentence. The house styles of some publishers may specify the "three dot" option (i.e., without the period). In the absence of any such instructions, you should go with the "four dot" treatment. **PD**

Layout and Design

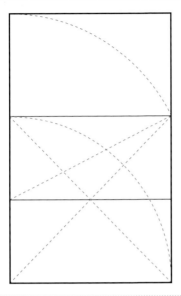

Thou shall learn about the Golden Section

Commentary Back when printed books were a relatively new idea, type was generally set in a single justified column and placed symmetrically on a spread with the outer margins wider than the inner, and the bottom margin deeper than the top. The proportions assigned to the text area were invariably worked out using a geometrical construct, the most highly regarded of these being the Golden Section. Measurements don't need to be specific as the resultant golden rectangle can be drawn without a ruler, using a set-square and compass.

The only important measurement is the ratio of short to long side, that being 1:1.618, which in itself doesn't really mean anything unless you're into ratios. This ratio occurs many times in art and architecture, so it was a natural choice for the basis of book layouts. The page's margins were often worked out using the Fibonacci sequence (0, 1, 1, 2, 3, 5, 8, 13, 21, and so on) which you can find out about by reading *The Da Vinci Code*. The explanation is quite near the start, so fortunately you don't have to read the whole thing. **TS**

088

Thou shall not be intimidated by a blank page

Commentary This is it. Everything you have trained for, all of your dreams and desires, the full realization of your creative potential awaits you. So why are your knees buckled and your hands shaking? It is just a blank page before you, a barren canvas for your skills to shape to your liking (or even better still, to the client's liking). Yet, it stands out as one of the most intimidating forces that a designer can ever face. No guides to go by, no style sheets deciding our typefaces and sizes for us. No corporate color palette already set out. No images already selected for inclusion. All of the decisions have been left up to us, and the pressure has left all parts of our body paralyzed. Pull yourself together!!! The opportunity for greatness lies before you. You are ready for this. I just know it. Look that blank page square in the eye and announce to the world that you are an incredible designer. Ready. Set. Go! **JF**

089

Thou shall triple check your document size before you start your layout

Commentary In the two decades I've been working as a graphic designer, I've heard a number of horror stories whereby a designer has worked to the wrong document size (for balance, the client, too, has got it wrong on occasion!). It's always discovered at that crucial stage during final approval after months of labor, or worse, when it's at the printers. This can of course be fixed, but it will cause a lot of stress: the client will be angry and there could be a cost issue or even a missed deadline. Also, the beautiful design that you have worked ever so hard on will have to be "bashed" hurriedly into shape, which could result in a poor-quality final product. Be as certain as possible from the start: check with the client the document size you are to work to and get it in writing, either on a contract or confirmed by email, in order to be sure of avoiding such problems. **PD**

Thou shall utilize master pages

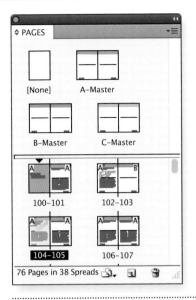

Commentary One of the huge advantages of using DTP software such as InDesign or QuarkXPress when laying out large documents is the master pages feature. With master pages you can preset all the consistent and repetitive elements that would appear on a page (running head, folios, heading boxes, text boxes, etc.) so that you don't have to keep recreating them every time you add a page. In addition, any alterations made to the masters will automatically be carried through to the pages you are working on, saving hours of labor-intensive activity and

ensuring there are no errors. As soon as you drop the master pages onto your "pages" palette window, you can be sure that the elements you need will be there, allowing you to concentrate on the layouts. You can also create differing masters for alternative grid designs within the same document and automatically renumber folios if you move spreads around. Even better, controlling your artworks with a "book" file allows you to update master pages across differing files without even opening them. Don't ignore them, they'll save you hours of work! **PD**

Thou shall use a grid

to maintain a layout's structure

Commentary Many designers rebel at the idea of using grids. They argue that the grid is there to punish them, limit creativity, and restrain freedom. In fact, the opposite is true. Grids celebrate harmonious proportions. They exist to create consistencies in negative and positive space. They allow the reader to know where to look for specific types of information. They are not to restrain the elements, but to create harmony. Consider a grid to be the same as the I-beam structure of a skyscraper. The I-beams give the structure strength, and allow for windows, doors, and individual rooms to relate with each other. In design, the grid is the invisible structure that unifies a poster, book, or website. Without a grid, any design solution becomes a hodgepodge of discord. There is one caveat, however, for those who are experts at grid usage. Grids are like spiderwebs. They should be pristine, elegant, and strong. But they are activated when one thing interrupts them. **SA**

Thou shall build visual pace into book and brochure layouts

Commentary If your next assignment is a 16-page brochure, visual pace won't be such a big priority, but if you're designing a 256-page illustrated book, this rule is for you. There are some types of books or brochures (or indeed websites) which demand that certain elements appear consistently from one spread to the next. For example, instructional books with illustrated tutorials (or perhaps books of graphic design rules) are likely to feature repeat page structures to aid navigation. However, for publications with content which varies throughout, seeing the same size image with the same amount of text and a caption in the same position every time could become very monotonous by the time you get past the first dozen spreads. Try to vary a layout from one spread to the next so images change size and position, thus allowing the flow of the text to meander and interact with the imagery in a more random fashion. Be careful not to lose navigability— the text and images must maintain a cordial relationship—but always build in as much pace as the material will support. **TS**

093

Thou shall understand how to design with a modular grid

Commentary We are going to learn an awful lot about designing with grids during our days doing layout, but one of the most useful is the modular grid. Like many things the Swiss masters brought into vogue, the modular grid is simple, yet deceivingly sophisticated, and incredibly intelligent. Formed using consistent horizontal divisions from top to bottom, in addition to vertical divisions from left to right, it determines where various elements and blocks of text line up. The result can be very simple or it can become terribly complex. The joy is that it will hold together through limitless variations. Sticking to the grid will create an invisible sense of balance among all elements on the layout, even as an image runs the width of three columns of a block of text the height of four. Even though you cannot see the lines in the final product, they pull it all together and the viewer just feels comfortable interacting with your work. **JF**

Thou shall break out of the grid if the layout prescribes it

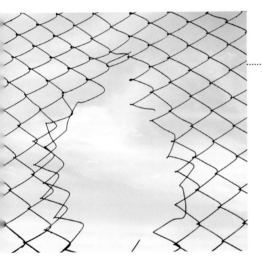

Commentary Grids are things of wonder to us designers, especially when they go all multi-column and modular. Exciting stuff! There's a saying that proclaims, "Behind every great man there stands a great woman," just as behind every great layout there stands a great grid. If it wasn't for those grids our layouts would stay out late drinking too much and end up lying in inconsistent gutters covered with messy typography. But hey, it's good for a layout to let its hair down every once in a while and give itself a break. Grids provide layouts with a stabilizing influence but a layout should take its grid out on the town every so often to say thanks for all that good advice. It's at times like these that the combination of perfect grid and flexible layout can make the grandest of statements. Without them, the life of a layout can become so phone directory, if you know what I mean? Okay— I just need to ask my wife to approve this text before I email it to the publisher. **TS**

Thou shall not automatically use the default margins in your layout program

Commentary As a "designer," the clue is in the title! You need to design, which means considering every minuscule aspect of any project you will be working on, including the margins. When considering the page layout, and how the content is going to be organized and structured within it, a part of your design process will be to develop a grid that works harmoniously with the page size. One of the grid's many structural components will be the margin area and you should consider applying a principle such as the Golden Section, described earlier in Rule #87, when deciding on its size and proportions. The default margins for new documents are just a standard border of $^1/_2$ inch or 12.7mm —almost a safety area for the complete novice— and have no design or structural merit, so think creatively and independently! This book uses inner and outer margins of $^7/_{10}$ inch/17.5mm with a top margin of 80.5pt and a bottom margin of 65.5pt. **PD**

$^1/_2$"
12.7mm

$^1/_2$"
12.7mm

Thou shall not place content too near the trim edge or gutter

Commentary Apart from an improvement in the tolerances involved, the technology used to trim and bind printed publications hasn't really changed much for decades. Even the best bindery plant has to account for some leeway when trimming finished copies of brochures and books, and for this reason it's advisable not to place content too near a trim edge. The fact that it might get guillotined off during the binding process is only half the story. It's harder to detect small changes in the gap between the text area and the trim if the said gap is generous enough to absorb a slight variance in width or height. Overly narrow margins will visibly "jump" if the pages of a book are thumbed rapidly, so try to allow at least ¼ inch (6mm) for small items like folios and at least twice that for large text blocks and images. Consider the gutter margin, too, as bunching may occur in publications with a large page extent, swallowing content which can otherwise only be seen by breaking the book's spine. **TS**

097

Thou shall design books and magazines as spreads, with facing pages

Commentary Walk into your closet and place a shirt against a pair of pants you are going to wear later in the week. Inevitably, you are going to want them to look decent against one another. Then take the shirt out and place it on the bed. A few hours later, walk into the closet and hold up a pair of pants against a shirt you wore yesterday. Again, you are going to want them to look good together. Put the pants on along with the shirt you laid out earlier. You know what doesn't match? Your hideous outfit! You would never dress this way, so why would you design a page in printer's spreads (already imposed) or worse, all alone? You know that the left and right facing pages will be next to one another for the final viewer, so start from that perspective when designing. Always consider what each what will appear on the opposite side to the page you're designing. **JF**

Thou shall design spreads with crossovers in mind

Commentary Now that we have decided to design with our pages facing one another (as anyone with common sense would), we have to consider the work that needs to be done after we have finished. Oh, right, the poor printers that have to realize our vision on paper and all bound up, allowing for pages to be turned and enjoyed. We know that the viewer will experience the pages side by side—in a spread— so we are designing with that in mind. We also know that it doesn't actually come together that way, that except for the center spread, none of the pages that nestle next to one another actually exist that way for the printer (thus, the designation "printer spreads" for the formation post imposition.) So we have to remember that letters that cross over from page to page will get cut off and not line up, images with specific detail will suffer the same fate. Some printers are better than others, but the onus is on us as designers to make it look its best. **JF**

099

Thou shall create a focal point for every layout

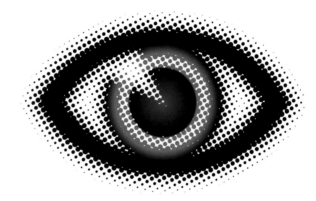

Commentary In most cases a layout will contain a piece of information such as a headline which should be the first thing the reader looks at. In Western culture the focal point is normally the top left corner of a page or spread, so it's no surprise that this is where a heading is usually positioned. Placing it anywhere else will fight against the natural instincts of the reader to look at the top left corner first. If you want to break away from this convention, and it's good to break the rules sometimes, the focus must be achieved using a visual device such as color, font size, or a strong graphic element. Bear in mind that readers tend to react in a different way to text and images as we're naturally inclined to gather information about what we're looking at, so a well-positioned headline will often trump an image in terms of focus. **TS**

Typography for the People 21

Thou shall always have at least one folio showing per spread

Commentary When you are deep in a design, it can be easy to lose sight of the final viewer. This leads to a number of different decisions, but one of the easiest to shed is the tiny, harmless little folio often at the bottom of the page. It's not really bothering anything, but my spread would look so nice if it had a clean section of deep color in the bottom left corner, and over here to the right seems to beg to go all white and, well, can't we just eliminate them for a spread? Certainly this works in the isolation of designing a single spread, but if we give in once, we are sure to do so a few more times before finishing off our publication. Now, the viewer doesn't interact with a single spread. They have the entire thing, well over a hundred pages in their hands and they like to know where they are as they flip through. You see what I am hinting at. They don't need to be on every page, but at least one of each facing one. **JF**

Thou shall periodically check a printed laser or inkjet rather than viewing a layout on screen

Commentary Despite the amazing quality and definition of modern monitors, there's nothing better to judge the quality and detailing in your design than viewing a printout at actual size. I always insist, when reviewing the earlier development stages of work in my studio, that we do it with laser printouts. Only then can we get the most accurate understanding of how the design is progressing, check the balance and structure of the layouts, the detailing and sizing of the typography, and check that all the content required for the page has been included. We still always start with paper and pen and never design on the screen. A majority of the time, your mind is concentrating on the mechanical aspects of using the software rather than the creative part of how to work the layouts. Only printouts will really show how your design is working. **PD**

Thou shall consider how a layout looks at full size and as a thumbnail online

Commentary I like small type as much as the next guy. All things being equal, I like it more than the next guy! I love a detailed and nuanced illustration or photo as well, something that truly rewards closer inspection. And I have come to realize that there is a time and a place for this type, but often that place is not in commercial products, even if it is a piece of music packaging that is only manufactured in a limited edition of a few hundred—certainly not on a book cover that will sell all around the world, or a can of soda that will be produced in the billions. Why, you ask. Why can't those layouts have little bits of important type? Because more often than not, they sell online, and that means respecting that most consumers will first interact with it in a tiny form. Be sure that it works both on screen and in person. **JF**

103

Thou shall use a baseline grid for body copy, especially in books and brochures

Commentary Let's quash a vicious rumor once and for all: baseline grids are not dull devices that restrict creativity. It's true that the "Why not just place everything where it looks right?" approach can work perfectly well for many projects, but if you're designing a brochure, magazine, or book, a baseline grid is an incredibly good idea. So if you've not used one before, you should give it a go. A baseline grid extends the standard row and column grid that most designers use to guide the placement of larger elements in a layout, providing a modular system that works both horizontally and vertically. Baseline grids encourage consistency because they help you to make decisions about where to position type and images across multiple pages, hence the reference to books and magazines earlier, and your layouts will look much more professional if repeat items such as page headings align properly throughout. **TS**

Thou shall take care to align baselines of type in adjacent columns

baseline baseline

Commentary You spend hours picking out just the right suit, spending a small fortune. You decide you can save a little bit on the tailoring, so you go to a cut-rate place around the corner. The day of the big event, you hustle back to get dressed only to discover that something looks a bit off in the mirror. Could it be that they have hemmed the pant legs a little higher on one leg compared to the other? You look at every angle, and it certainly appears so. Nothing major you think, who would notice such a thing, anyway. You jet off and soon find yourself standing outside the dance floor. A very attractive woman comes up and asks if you are "able to dance." You flash an uneasy smile and reply, "Don't you mean would I like to dance?" "No," she says. "I meant are you able? On account of your legs being two different lengths." **JF**

105

Thou shall align the bottom margin with the baseline grid

Commentary This is one of my pet favorites when it comes to rules that should never be broken (yep, there are some unbreakable rules). That doesn't stop designers from doing it though, and when they do, it highlights one of the worst possible layout errors, the *slight* misalignment. Here's the scenario. The margins are set and the baseline grid is added with a start point at the top of the text area. All good to go you say but wait—the final baseline and the bottom margin don't quite line up because the margins are in inches and the baseline grid is in points. This is such an easy thing to put right as all you have to do is measure the final baseline to trim distance in either of those units and set that as your bottom margin. But so many folks don't bother and it looks so messy when you try to align an image with the last line of text. The funny thing is, slight misalignments really stand out while whopping great big ones don't because they look intentional. Please avoid. **TS**

Thou shall align layout content harmoniously

Commentary Alignment considerations should extend to all elements of a layout taken as a whole rather than simply images with images, text with text, and so on. Furthermore, the alignment of the text itself should be considered alongside the positioning of images, so an image centered on a page might benefit from a centered headline beneath it. If you want to draw the reader's attention toward a premium image positioned toward the right of a brochure spread, consider using flush right text aligned down the left edge, but be careful not to propel the reader's eye off the spread altogether. The way elements align within any layout influences the structure just as much as the grid dictates where content should be placed, and as long as the elements don't fight with one another while jostling for position, a layout will generally work perfectly well. The harmony in a layout stems not from the fact that alignments are right, but from the fact that they're not wrong. **TS**

Thou shall not always attempt to align captions to the same baseline as body copy

Examples of unspoilt medieval architecture can be found throughout the Limousin region of central France.

French ar
followed a
with empl
A growing
but one m
In the Do
with mucl
but of fine
neighborii
pioneer of
Several fa
and it is r
natural st
pale color

Commentary It's a common error among inexperienced designers, as they try to get a grip on the "rules" of using page and baseline grids, to become obsessed with locking everything to grids, including captions. This doesn't need to be the case. At the start of a project, as you evaluate the content supplied and decide on the styling requirements, you will have to decide which text elements should be locked to the grid. As your body text is larger than the captions, the leading applied to it (which your baseline grid has been set to) will be too great for the captions. This will result in them looking aesthetically poor and "gappy." You can, however, set the first line of the caption to lock to the baseline grid so that it is in alignment with the top line of the body text. With this done, it's simply a case of applying an appropriate leading to the caption and letting it hang. **PD**

Thou shall use alternative baseline grids within caption boxes

The magenta keylines drawn above the master baseline grid help to demonstrate how selecting an alternative baseline grid for your caption boxes allows you to align body and caption text with different leading.

Commentary An alternative to the technique outlined in Rule #107 is to create your own custom baseline grid for captions. This is particularly useful when your page layout has multiple captions (such as annotation) spread across the two pages. DTP software such as InDesign allows you to create adjustable baseline grids within the caption boxes, independent from the baseline set on your master pages. This allows you to ensure alignment between captions if the boxes are positioned correctly. It also allows you to create a ratio between the two baseline grids so you can create a proportionate leading between the two text styles. For example, say your page leading is set at 15pt with 10pt body text. Your captions can be set at 10pt leading with 7pt body text, giving a multiple of three lines for every two from the master baseline grid. If you align the first line of your caption text with any line of the body text, your typography will look much sweeter! **PD**

109

Thou shall use rounded numerical values when placing elements on your layout

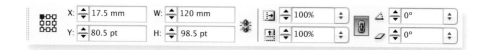

X: 17.5 mm W: 120 mm 100% 0°
Y: 80.5 pt H: 98.5 pt 100% 0°

Commentary "Graphic designer" and "typographer" should be bywords for precision, and a compulsion to be accurate is essential when working with type and layouts on a computer. After all, your project will be printed or published online for everybody to see. One of my real pet hates (and it REALLY drives me mad!) is the inaccurate laying out and positioning of elements for artwork, such as employing random and inconsistent measurements throughout. For example, a picture box positioned 10.367mm from the top of the trim edge—what's wrong with 10mm? A picture scaled to 86.428 percent— why not 86.5 percent? Headlines at 30.697pt—where did that figure come from? I understand we all have a lot to think about and a lot to remember (the numerous rules in this book are prime examples), and invariably with a deadline looming the pressure is on, but taking care with your work brings more quality to it and will make you the better designer. Phew! Okay, rant over . . . . **PD**

Thou shall ensure spacing is consistent throughout a layout

Visit our private beach   *Relax in style*   *Check out the surf*   *Remember a good book*

Commentary Rigor is part of the job of being a good designer. It is the difference between a world-class designer and a hack. Sloppy and inconsistent spacing is the first clue to identifying a careless designer. First, use a grid to maintain consistent line length, rule width, and image sizes. Second, use the guides to ensure uniformity in the position of text and images. Third, specify a comfortable distance between the baseline of a caption and the bottom of an image. Adhere to this spacing on all images. Fourth, create rules (stroke size) as part of the paragraph style of the text. This will maintain a consistent spacing between the baseline of the typography and the rule. It may be tempting to optically determine these spacing issues, but you are not that good. Do it mathematically and consistently. **SA**

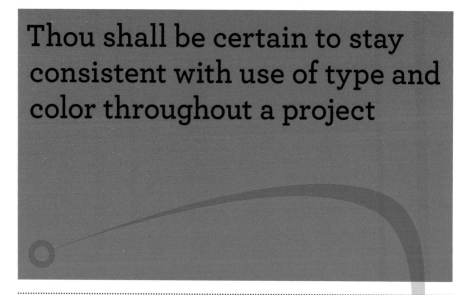

111

Thou shall be certain to stay consistent with use of type and color throughout a project

Commentary There are two schools of design. At one extreme of the spectrum designers believe that self-expression with no regard to the client problem is "good design." At the other end of the spectrum are designers who believe that the individual designer's style should be invisible and only the client's problem should be relevant. Many designers work somewhere between both schools, solving a problem, while allowing for self-expression. Unless a designer is only interested in self-expression, with no regard to communication, consistency of typographic style, and color palette is required. Basic compositional rules dictate that a color palette be related, and each color echoed somewhere on the project. A design solution calls for a large red circle. Echo this color elsewhere, so it does not appear to be an alien object. The same is true with typography. Univers is the typeface on the cover of a book. Use Univers inside the book also. Otherwise it will appear that two different designers, with no communication, designed the cover and interior. **SA**

Hello. I am Important.

**I am also important. Not as important
as the item on the top though.**

I am required reading but not essential.

I am secondary information that would be nice
if you read me and comprehended my deeper
understanding of the subject matter.

- I am bulleted text. Highlighted.
- I am also bulleted text. Highlighted.
- I am also bulleted text. Highlighted.
- I am still bulleted text. Highlighted.

Thou shall establish a visual hierarchy which leads to the most important information

Commentary Assembling all of the components for your design is the easy part. Making sure to get the main point across is much more difficult. The first, and most important step is to establish what that point is with your client. Once you are on the same page, the sooner you start to set up a hierarchy, the easier time you will have in creating a successful solution. There is always a "star" or "hero"—the most important bit of information that the viewer should take away. Be sure that your layout, right down to your font selections and type size, all reflect this goal. It can be as simple as size or placement, but often you will need to dig into your toolbox for color and other graphic devices. You will then need to work out which is the next most important bit and so on and so on. Using everything you know about type and image, set up your layout so that the viewer leaves with all of the needed information. **JF**

113

Thou shall experiment with paragraph layout only for conceptual emphasis

This was the point in the story when an INTENSE flash took him over and sent things *sprawling, falling, crawling,* seemingly all was lost as he began to choke.

The other side, *reaching* out, was a light. Dim, then brighter and brighter still. Until he knew that he had properly laid out the paragraph.

Commentary After all of this talk about rules, it is probably starting to feel like all we are telling you is things that you can't do. The man is literally keeping you down. I thought we all got into this to be creative, right? Well, here is a bit of freedom of the highest order. Now that you know the rules, and you know that most other professionals have a fair grasp on the major ones as well, you can finally break them wide open. Nothing makes a bigger impact on a reader than an experimental layout of a paragraph, or set of paragraphs. The key is that it has to be intentional and purposeful, or else it will just look shoddy and unprofessional. A layout about a dense forest gets six tall, narrow columns of type nearly side by side? Worth looking in to! A story about reaching a mountaintop is laid out in a cone of type widening with each line? You know it works. Just be sure to only do it when really and truly appropriate. **JF**

Thou shall not ignore the advantages of visual grouping

Commentary Imagine if you could take a layout and physically pull it apart in several different directions. If there's no strong relationship bonding the elements that make up the layout it'll split and pull apart, but if you've used visual grouping effectively the layout will spring back together like elastic when you let go. It's a slightly odd analogy, I know, but think it through and you'll see what I mean. Using visual grouping will provide structure for a layout that might otherwise appear as a collection of free-floating islands.

Grouping anchors objects together by invisible threads, which our eyes then fill in for us, and in turn help to create good navigation by drawing the eye through a layout in the correct order. Grouping can be achieved through the use of borders, panels, rules, or even typographic hierarchy, as well as the obvious idea of using proximity to form distinct groups of content. Take care not to create areas of trapped space between groups by watching what's happening around the edges of your layout. **TS**

Thou shall not corral white space in the middle of a layout

Commentary When designers talk about white space, what they really mean is blank paper. If you're new to graphic design, you might feel uneasy about white space, seeing it as a missed opportunity to add another image or some more text. The thing is, the white space between items is integral to a layout's structure for two reasons. Firstly, it provides a frame for objects or groups, thus setting them apart from other elements. Secondly, it helps to create better visual navigation by drawing a reader's eye through a layout in the correct sequence. For both these reasons you should try to avoid creating blocks of white space which are surrounded on all sides, as these areas of white space act like holes in a layout which the reader can fall in to and get stuck. Try to give your white space room to breathe and don't pen it in or it'll turn on you and do bad things to your layout. **TS**

Thou shall only use as many columns as you genuinely need

Commentary A document grid exists to make it easier to create accurate layouts with correctly and consistently positioned content, so it makes sense to keep grids simple. A good grid will also be flexible, of course, as you don't want to be restricted by what you can do with the content, and the number of columns you use exerts considerable influence on that flexibility. Grids with odd numbers of columns can be particularly useful as they allow images to break into columns of text and you can vary the measures for running text, captions, and so on without departing from the grid itself. However, try not to get carried away with the number of columns you introduce. A 27-column grid is all very well, but it's very hard to keep track of consistency with that many columns in use and you're likely to end up with columns that are equal to or narrower than the gutters. Start with fewer columns and add more as required, or use guides to create sub-columns if you need them. **TS**

Thou shall persevere with InDesign's Table functionality

Commentary Early in my career I worked for a design firm that did a lot of work for the tourism industry, so that meant brochures with lots of complex price tables created "by hand" in QuarkXPress®. All the rows and columns were separately drawn rules and all the text was tabbed by hand or a series of individually linked text boxes. Boy, was it difficult and time-consuming work, but what a sense of achievement when you'd completed a table with all the footnotes and extras.

Until, that is, the client calls to say they need to "add three weeks to the season and oh, by the way, we secured rooms in two more hotels." Without table functionality it's start again—no going home for you tonight, my friend. With table functionality, it's "insert two columns" and "insert three rows," adjust the size a little, and you're off to a bar for a well-deserved beer. It's not that intuitive a process to be honest, but it's worth sticking with in case you ever get that call. **TS**

Thou shall only use footnotes* where they best serve the editorial content

Commentary When you are considering typographic styling for a book, it may be that the use of marginal annotation is requested by the author or client. If so, stop and consider what type of book or publication it is and what the comments are actually communicating. If working on a technical or academic title, it will be useful to employ the annotation as "footnotes" (i.e., at the bottom of the page) to aid the reader and expand on their understanding of the material.

If these footnotes are more reference-based (for example, a list of third-party reference material) then these could be placed at the rear of the book as "endnotes." Similarly, if a large volume of footnotes exists and the title is more of a narrative text, as in a story, then an abundance of footnotes placed at the bottom of the page can look unsightly, be intimidating to read, and may break up the flow too much. Better that these are placed as "endnotes," as previously described. **PD**

*An ancillary item of text providing additional information that is printed at the foot of the page.

119

Thou shall remember that one does not have to fill up every section of a multi-column page

Commentary White space is your friend. Say it with me. White space is my friend. Like in music, it is often the notes that you don't play that resonate the most with the listener. Far too many layouts suffer from crowding out, filling every last nook and cranny with elements or text. Say you have a multi-column layout before you, and the text holds to the style of the rest of the document. But paired with the photo and caption on the page, it leaves enough space for two more paragraphs.

The compulsion can be to increase the size of the photo until it all fills out the space perfectly. Worse still, you might start adding extra spot illustrations or pumping up the size of a pull quote to force the issue. All of that takes away from the original intent and ends up making the layout uncomfortably crowded. The grid already has the page organized and less is often more. **JF**

This is one column of text that you need to deal with. Factor in the length and start planning.

This is one column of text that you need to deal with. Factor in the length and start planning. How you decide to use this, now that you know it will be longer, determines a lot.

This is one column of text that you need to deal with.

This is one column of text that you need to deal with. Why not try a hangline?

Thou shall consider a hangline when given inconsistent columns of text

Commentary One of the most maddening things can be when a designer is presented with inconsistent amounts of text that need to work in a multi-column document. But a little perspective helps soothe the nerves and find a ready solution. When you are given a stack of framed prints to go across a wall and they all differ in height, what do you do? You make a horizontal line where the tops of each piece start at the same distance from the ceiling so that you have a clear visual organization that celebrates the difference in scale, while still keeping the wall from feeling cluttered and all akimbo. The same is true in a layout. Creating a hangline, you organize the vertical columns with a horizontal line in your grid. You can even have certain elements only exist above the line, etc. It is referred to as a hangline because the columns of text "hang" from a common line invisible to the viewer. **JF**

Thou shall use layers to organize type, color, and imagery

Commentary The ability to organize and distribute content over a range of separate layers that can be color coded and labeled is an absolute no-brainer. It's one of the best things introduced into today's layout applications. So it's a bit of a mystery why anyone wouldn't use layers, instead choosing to dump everything onto one default layer. What happens if you want to select something that appears behind another object? Lots of fiddling about and multiple clicking—that's what. Sure, it's not essential for simple layouts that only get worked on by you, but what if you work with a team or have to send files out for third parties to edit. The ability to add all the text to its own layer and lock up the color so it can't be moved or deleted accidentally is a pretty compelling argument. Try to get into the habit of using at least one extra layer for all your text and it'll pay dividends in the long run. **TS**

Thou shall not use multiple layers of content unless they provide a benefit

Commentary First, let me define layers here. This is not the good type of layer a designer uses to organize information with Adobe® Photoshop®. This is the result of reckless layering of objects, images, and typography to create interest. Interestingly, this same technique of layering images on top of other images, or pieces of typography, was an afternoon hobby of upper-class women in Victorian England and 19th-century America. Hopefully, a century of technological advances, aesthetic movements, and educated designers, has discarded this technique in favor of clear communication. Unfortunately, there are still designers who are under the false assumption that they have invented a unique and revolutionary style with layers on layers of found images, odd squiggles, and distorted typography. Too often, when faced with a project that isn't compelling, a designer decides that adding another element will help. This is wrong. This is the same as putting more frosting on a badly made cake. Go back to square one; the original idea is probably flawed. Adding to it is only ignoring the reality of a bad idea. **SA**

123

Thou shall not use Microsoft Word for layouts

Commentary If I had a dollar for every client who, fancying themselves as something of a designer, has used Word to lay out a document, I would be a rich man! So why not use it? Well, Word provides little flexibility for a designer to work with as it is set up for writing letters, making lists, or laying out text-based reports. The clue is in the name: it is great for writing text, not designing layouts. For the graphic designer, Word's very limited page layout and typographic features do not allow any flexibility, or the precision to craft and create designs. In addition, Word has no prepress ability, nor does it have industry standards such as Pantone color systems built in. You should be using dedicated design software such as InDesign® or QuarkXPress® for your work. You wouldn't use a saw to hammer a nail into wood, so don't use Word to design your layouts. Ever! **PD**

Thou shall not design in PowerPoint

....

Commentary You might think I am crazy for even making this a rule, but trust me when I tell you that sooner rather than later a client will be asking you to design something in PowerPoint, all the while swearing up and down that it is the most creative application ever created and you just haven't tried to appreciate its abilities. Now, we can acknowledge that PowerPoint may indeed be the most creative application that THEY have ever worked in. But we have other tools at our disposal. PowerPoint is good at one thing and one thing only, making incredibly basic slide shows. And even there, it is horribly out of date. What it has in its favor is that it is used everywhere, thus the push from your client. Frighteningly, its tools seem to have been set up to encourage crimes against design, particularly when it comes to scaling type and images vertically. I shudder just thinking about it. Don't encourage it and certainly don't do it yourself. **JF**

125

Thou shall learn how to thread large quantities of linked text correctly

Commentary Let me paint a picture here. A designer receives copy for a publication. He or she places the copy into the Adobe® InDesign® document. The designer then copies and pastes each paragraph into place. So far, everything seems okay. The client reviews the proof and changes the order of the pages. The copy is now no longer in the same order in which it was first supplied, and the designer has no idea where each paragraph should subsequently belong. This is bad. Alternatively, once copy is placed in the document and organized as linked, or threaded, text, the order will always remain clear. By selecting "show text threads" handy arrows appear. These identify each text block and the order of subsequent text blocks. **SA**

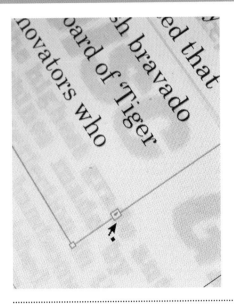

Thou shall create text threads for stories or chapters at the planning stage

Commentary When you are first supplied with the copy for a multi-page layout, you are usually forced to break it up into parts to a certain degree, but large portions can usually stay intact. It is best to keep stories or chapters as a single chunk of copy by first importing the text into a series of threaded text boxes. The small signifier at the bottom right of the first text box can be clicked to load the cursor with any overmatter, allowing you to create as many extra text boxes as needed to

view the complete linked text chain. Once all the copy is styled, you will know how many pages it takes up and be able to start making some design decisions pretty quickly. Why is this preferable to creating separate text boxes and cutting and pasting each item of copy as you go? Because subsequent edits will affect the entire flow of the story or chapter, and losing that connection is the quickest and easiest way to misplace a portion of text in your final file. **JF**

127

Thou shall always spell-chcek—especially when text is suplied

Commentary Many designers believe they are visual people and reading is for uptight academics only. Or they are convinced that spelling in the texting world is correct. This is wrong. "You're" is not spelled "UR." The mark of an ignorant and careless person is most clearly illuminated by misspelling. Nothing is more detrimental than spelling errors in a proposal, email, or presentation. A misspelling on a résumé is, frankly, a career-killer. In the past, a keen eye and superior education solved this issue. Today, *spell-chec*k is the solution. The same rules apply to copy supplied by the client. The initial contract should make clear that all copy proofing is the final responsibility of the client. However, once a project is printed or published online, a misspelled word remains a sign of carelessness. The designer will be assigned the blame as he or she sets the copy. This may lead to the designer paying for a rerun of the entire job, or any damages caused by the error. Once again, spell-checking the copy, regardless of the source, is the easy and required solution. **SA**

Thou shell note rely solely on the spell-checker two prick up every text error

Commentary Every designer should possess a dictionary in support of any computer-based spell-checking software. It's a must! Spell-checkers are far from perfect, and, as illustrated in our rule above, they will not highlight words that are spelled correctly but out of context. International spelling creates further issues. If you are reading this book in the United States you will not find anything out of the ordinary with the spelling, but British readers will notice, for example, an abundance of the letter "z" where there would normally be an "s." This book is an international co-edition with U.S. spelling, but because many words have two acceptable spelling variations, and with spell-checkers defaulting to a U.S. preference, it is always worthwhile checking with the client to see which style they prefer to use for their publications and whether they can provide guidelines. **PD**

Thou shall not rekey supplied text into a layout—always copy and paste

Commentary On occasion we work with manuscripts that are up to 100,000 words long. That's a lot of content written by an author, edited by a client, and sometimes revisited by a proofreader. The manuscript has been checked, amended, and finalized—and is correct! We therefore always copy and paste the texts into a layout and never rekey in—even if we think it's saving time or is an easy word—as even the shortest of words has the chance to be misspelt by retyping.

If you do rekey in and make a mistake, the client will spot it, wonder how this mistake has occurred, and be annoyed that you introduced errors into their material. They might then mistrust you as a supplier and wonder what other errors you could possibly have made. Worse still, they might not spot the error until the book has printed! That's not good for any client–designer relationship. It is more than just a typo—it's all about trust, respect, and being professional. **PD**

Thou shall understand how and why a book or brochure publication is structured

Commentary As with letterform anatomy, so with books and brochures—it is important to know how they are structured. A book, or other publication type, has many elements to it other than the cover and text pages. The designer must be familiar with these details, as they have to be factored into the flatplan and designed in the appropriate manner. Items such as the half-title and title pages, the imprint and contents, are integral to book publishing and it would be embarrassing if you had to ask the client what they are! There are, of course, certain orthodoxies in the running order of a book, especially within the prelims and endmatter. These vary depending on content, but they all work to more or less the same structure. However, once you know the naming conventions and the standards, you can explore how to present them in fun and exciting ways. **PD**

131

Thou shall not use Paragraph Composer in InDesign®

Commentary *Paragraph Composer* is a feature (and the default setting) within InDesign® that automatically controls line breaks in paragraphs. Although it might be a useful feature for inexperienced designers, I would never use it in my work. Instead, you should always make certain it is switched to the alternative *Single-line Composer*. The single-line mode allows the designer to control line breaks and not have InDesign® making tracking and line-ending adjustments on your behalf. The central problem with Paragraph Composer is that, when making even the slightest adjustment, such as changing a word, the entire paragraph will reflow. If you have soft returns in the paragraph then this will cause further issues. For editors working on books, it's just a nightmare. Work on the text completed previously can be undone by a piece of auto-formatting prompted by Paragraph Composer, and gaps in the body text can open up without the editor's knowledge. As the designer, keep it single-line and make the line-ending adjustments yourself. As they say, no pain, no gain. **PD**

suggest

Thou shall ~~recommend~~ copy changes if they ~~can~~ improve clarity and help the layout

Commentary There are many ideas about the purpose of design. Some claim that it is in service of commerce, others postulate that it be used for social change. One side of the industry supports personal exploration, while the other encourages an impersonal approach. In any instance, the most basic requirement is communication. Clear communication is a result of legible and understandable visual forms. Designers are not "type maids." It is not the designer's job to take someone's messy content and clean it up. A good designer clarifies the content with visual form and copy. If the copy is unclear or just plain wrong, suggest changes. If the problem is extreme, suggest hiring a copywriter. The final product in its entirety reflects on the designer's skills. Saying, "I didn't have anything to do with the copy," will not enhance a designer's reputation. **SA**

133

Thou shall design website visuals to correct screen proportions

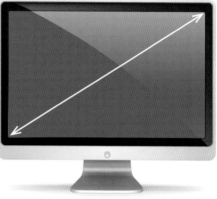

Commentary When asked to create a website concept, many designers use software they know well, say Photoshop or InDesign, before handing visuals over to a developer. If the design is going to translate successfully to the screen, it's really helpful to design to a page size that's correctly proportioned for the majority of screens so the developer can slice up the artwork without having to rejig everything. A safe bet for most screens is 1024 x 768 pixels, and a ratio of 1:0.75, which will cater to the majority of global users, although 1280 x 800 or 1:0.625 is actually slightly more popular in the U.S. and UK. This isn't the whole story, however, as users tend not to maximize their browser window, so it's a good idea to design for a fixed width while assuming that users will expect to scroll down to view more content. Research indicates that a fixed width of 960 pixels seems to be an acceptable size to go for. **TS**

134

Thou shall not employ a web developer who has a bad website

Commentary When we start to assemble a team for a project, we often don't heed our own advice. We expect that our clients will do their homework and research various designers and determine who might be the best fit for their particular project before giving us a call or email (because, we are indeed the perfect fit for them, of course.) When this doesn't take place, we are the first to throw a little fit. However, when we go looking for a writer, we often don't read their samples and worse yet, we choose web developers based on their price and availability, forgetting that they are going to be a creative partner in realizing our vision for the client. Think about it as if you were putting together a band. If you play hard rock and you need a bass player, you don't go hiring the guy playing in the horrific calypso band in the mall, just because he is free on Saturday nights. You already know he has lousy taste. Be as diligent with your own teammates. **JF**

135

Thou shall remember that type legibility differs wildly from print to screen

Commentary It seems like an obvious thing to say that what works in print won't necessarily work on screen, but let's say it anyway. A font like Times Roman is generally accepted as one of the most readable serifs in print, even if it lacks a little in style. However, it is an absolute failure onscreen, with its forms distorting and it being generally tough to understand. Screen legibility is most influenced by a typeface's x-height, so keep that as a consideration. Times New Roman has been adapted with a moderate x-height and works much better on screen. Certain typefaces have been constructed specifically with an on screen application in mind, like Georgia and Verdana, and we find them lacking in most respects in print form. The most important part of the equation is figuring out where your text is going to be read, and designing with that foremost in your mind. **JF**

Thou shall always use typographic style sheets in long documents

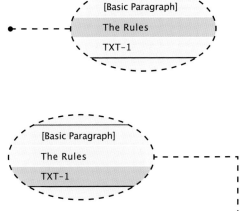

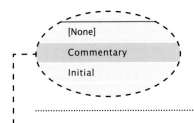

Commentary Style sheets are a thing of beauty and, when used correctly, will enhance your life and make you a better person! Well, maybe I'm going a bit far, but what they will do is provide exacting consistency and ensure that a number of fail-safes are in place when you are typesetting a long document such as a book. First, simply create the style sheet, incorporating every facet of styling needed— typeface, size, tracking, and so on. Highlight the text and click on the desired style in the Paragraphs style palette and, hey presto, all done! Consider the following situation: you're nearing the end of the book and the client asks to see the B-Heads one point bigger. It's a change you are happy to make as it's a single adjustment to the style master! The hundreds of B-Heads in the book are instantly restyled, saving you the pain of doing each one manually. Joy! **PD**

137

Thou shall always use object styles when working with long documents

Commentary As designers we tend to concentrate on the things we see directly in our layouts, so the type, color, images and so on. What we don't always think about with the right level of priority are the properties of the frames that contain those items, and the various rules and borders that make up the page furniture. Master pages are great for adding repeat content to the pages of a long document but a lot of additional content gets added along the way. Object styles containing information about a frames color, stroke thickness and even the text contained within can be applied in the same way that character and paragraph styles can be applied directly to selected type. This naturally helps to speed up your workflow and as a by-product helps to ensure consistency throughout a document. It's all too easy to start a project with 0.5pt rules that accidentally become 0.3pt rules half way through and these small details are very difficult to spot on screen. You can bet you'll spot it straight away when you see the printed item, so use object styles to achieve perfect consistency, just like peas in a pod! **TS**

Thou shall seduce your audience with your layout

Commentary The opposite of seduction is repulsion. When we use seduction in a bedroom, we use soft lights, play 101 Strings Orchestra albums, and offer alcohol. Turning on the overhead fluorescent lights, playing Anthrax, and offering heroin may be repulsing, depending upon the date. Design is no different. Good design seduces the viewer. The message might be complex, controversial, or challenging, but the viewer must be willing to view it. Creating work that is, at first glance, impossible to access and repulsive to everyone fails. Seduce the audience. Utilize pleasant colors, legible typography, and clear imagery. Consider Andy Warhol's *Electric Chair* series. Silk-screened with vibrant and optimistic tones, these paintings hang on walls above sofas. They look beautiful, but they are a discourse on death and execution. This does not mean that every project should be "pretty." We can be seduced by strong images and dark tones. Confused and impossible-to-access work will repulse. The viewer has limited time and will instantly decide which solution to engage or ignore. **SA**

139

Thou shall follow Coco Chanel's advice, "When accessorizing, always take off the last thing you put on."

Commentary Too much of a good thing is still too much. When dressing, you may have a box of beautiful Rolex, Cartier, and Tiffany watches. Wearing them all at once does not increase the overall effect. This looks like Madonna in the 1980s. Designing a poster, book, website, or any other item is the same. More is not more. If an element is purely decorative and serves no purpose, then it serves no purpose. It is a distraction at best. Good design is purposeful. Every typeface, image, ornament, shape, and color must have a reason to be. When we fall in love with our own design, it is easy to ignore the extra, unnecessary items. A good practice, like Coco Chanel's advice, is to take one element off when you are finished with the design. **SA**

Thou shall not assume small adjustments will improve a bad layout

Commentary The core of good time management understands the time needed to complete a task, and stopping when it is finished. Long hours and all-night sessions are typically the result of repeatedly adjusting small elements in a layout. Refinement is a different issue. When a designer refines a design, he or she finely crafts the typography, color, and form. The goal here is to create an immaculate solution, free from sloppy technique.

Small adjustments, shifting a line of text up 1 pica, down 1 pica, and back repeatedly, are done to attempt to solve a larger issue. This issue is probably a bad idea. If the basic concept is flawed, adjusting elements forever will not make it right. A great concept can withstand any layout issues. When a designer is making these tiny adjustments all night, he should stop, and ask, "Am I simply adding lipstick to a hog?" **SA**

Thou shall not use random squiggles and rules unless they actually mean something

Commentary Similar to the error of making small and pointless adjustments to a layout, is the issue of additive thinking. This is the scenario: The solution seems dull and bland. The designer adds several rules. It still is dull and the designer adds random hand-drawn squiggles. The dullness doesn't abate. More rules and squiggles are added. This process continues until the solution is, at first glance, "hip and now," but is in reality, a mess. It is all cake frosting on top of a hollow cake. In 1912, this process resulted in the moving of deck chairs as the Titanic sank. Today, this can be passed off as avant-garde design. It is not. True avant-garde work challenges our perceptions and ideas. Meaningless form is meaningless. **SA**

Thou shall use borders with a purpose, not simply for decoration

Commentary Borders are for more than just scrapbooking, that much is for sure, but they are not to be used without thoughtful consideration. Borders can be a wonderful element. They come in so many variations. Thick and thin, ornate and ragged, rough versus clean, they can allow the designer the ability to convey so much as well as to quite simply highlight a bit of important information or liven up a dull image or layout. Borders are our friends . . . when we use them properly. When we throw them up just for decoration, they often do more harm than good. If you have a garden that the rabbits are savaging (curses to you, long ear!) then a pretty pink fence with wide gaps between the slats certainly isn't going to keep them out, and what's the point in dressing up a patch of yard that has now turned into a barrage of holes and half-eaten carrots? The same holds true for your borders in your layout. **JF**

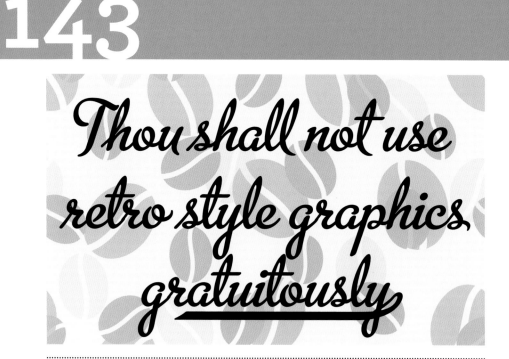

Thou shall not use retro style graphics gratuitously

Commentary Retro graphics are without doubt one of the most in-vogue styles in many current graphic design circles. The theory goes that the whole handmade thing is a reaction against all the pixel-perfect imagery which became so *de rigueur* with the advent of the digital design age, and retro styling provides a great excuse to use some inked texture or some grubby colors with headlines set in a bold calligraphic script. There are even dedicated apps and Photoshop® plug-ins to help you turn pristine artwork into a mis-registered screenprint or a facsimile of a cheaply printed comic book. Personally I love the whole retro deal, but I sometimes have to stop myself from trying to justify how I can create concepts which use retro styling at their center. If you're designing an indie poster for a band, or a book jacket for a cool new collection of urban fiction, then retro might be right on the button.But any attempt to bang any round peg of style into the square hole of appropriateness is probably not going to work out. **TS**

Thou shall design signage layouts to be read, not just seen

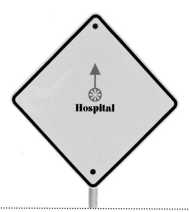

Commentary There are few designers who do not like small type. Rarely do clients ask to make the type or their logo smaller. Smaller type appears more delicate and provides more negative space, aesthetically appealing results. But type that is too small is not functional. Signs are a perfect example of this problem. Signage must be readable, not simply aesthetically appealing. In the midst of a fire, the viewer, even a designer, will not stop to appreciate the delicate typography and refined white space of an evacuation map—he or she just wants to find the stairs as fast as possible. This requires typography and iconography to be large enough to be read quickly, and from a distance. The contrast of the message on the background must be strong. The letterforms should be sharp and clear. Do not use degenerated, decorative, or overwrought typefaces. And the type size will always need to be larger than you think. There is good reason why street signs are not set in Curlz. **SA**

Thou shall design book covers with title readability as a priority

Commentary The best book cover designers will all readily acknowledge how important it is to keep readability intact. Many spend days judging how distressed they might be able to get a type solution, while still retaining readability. They will always err on the side of being able to comprehend it though. When you have music packaging, people hear things and have additional interactions; even major and minor brands of food and beverages have consumers tasting and experiencing their product. With books, people read: It is as simple as that. That's not to say that you can't take chances—by all means be creative. But always keep in mind that the title and author name need to be read; and in this digital sales age, that they need to be read at a very small scale in order to move enough units on Amazon so that the publisher can afford to pay your design bill. **JF**

Thou shall design logos that have mnemonic value

Commentary We remember stuff by recognizing shape and color. This is not an accident. As an evolutionary tool, as hunter–gatherers it was important to remember the blue berries were poisonous, but the oval red berries were good. We use this trait now still to recall the items we need. Rather than berries and fruits, the viewer now needs to identify products. Successful logos utilize our skill at recognizing shape and color. If a form is too complex, as an illustration or disjointed set of elements, it is difficult to recall. If a logo uses a banal color palette, or colors difficult to identify, such as puce, it may fail. Simple and clear forms with a distinct shape and color, therefore, have mnemonic value. Consider the Apple®, FedEx®, McDonald's®, and London Underground logos. Each of these has a distinct shape: a circle, rectangle and arrow, arch, and a circle and bar. Each of these also has a distinct and simple color: gray, purple and green, red and yellow, and red and navy blue. **SA**

Thou shall design logos that can adapt to a company's changing needs

Commentary Paul Rand introduced the IBM logo in 1956, and IBM continues to use his logo today. In 1956, IBM—known previously as International Business Machines Corporation—designed and produced computers and other business machines. Today, IBM is engaged in a range of activities from training and consulting to computers. If Rand had designed the IBM logo with an image of a Random Access Memory machine, today it would be stuck in the business of only making this product. A neutral logo allows a company to shift direction, change products, move into other categories, and still maintain its identity. A logo that is too specific to a product or activity presumes the company will never change. Good logos don't describe a company's activities, they identify its values. **SA**

Thou shall not ignore a client's corporate standards

Commentary Before the cultural revolution of the 1960s, people went to work in accounting, law, insurance, and manufacturing and did their job. They didn't consider themselves to be artists. Today, everyone is told to be "creative." Everyone should be unique and express him or herself. This works well when choosing ties, but is a recipe for disaster with corporate standards. These standards exist to maintain a clear, cohesive, and proprietary voice for a client. They are not created to restrain creativity simply as a measure of meanness. Within any company, people will want to ignore the standards and make their own logo or add purple because it is their favorite color. As a designer, you are collaborating with the enemy of you do the same. Save the need for creative expression for the concept, leave the logo, color, and typeface alone. **SA**

Thou shall create logos your client can use anywhere

ARTISAN

CONFECTIONS

Commentary A well-crafted logo is something that is built to last. It is crafted so that it can be applied to every application imaginable for the business it represents. Don't produce something that your client won't be able to use anywhere other than on their website. Logo designs that incorporate bitmaps are restrictive as they do not allow for unlimited scaling. While this excludes a feathered drop shadow from the discussion, I think we can all agree that is for the better. (Flip through the portfolios of the logo masters and let me know when you come across a drop shadow.) The reason that you need to try to avoid bitmapped logos at the onset is that even if you think the client may never need it, a wise branding exercise will be prepared for anything that comes next. Logos built with vectors can be scaled infinitely with no loss of quality. Logos that contain bitmaps cannot. If you need your logo properly embroidered on shirts, you need a vector version. If you need it silkscreened on recycling bins, you need a vector version. If you need it eight stories high on the side of a building, vector. **JF**

150

Thou shall understand the figure/ground relationship in logos

Commentary Logos are a two-dimensional exercise, and with anything 2D one must take into account the figure/ground relationship. Because, in most cases, it is centered around one strong image, it takes on a heightened importance in logo design. The figure part of the equation is essentially the object that we see, and the ground is the surrounding area. Applying contrast to make this relationship as obvious as is possible, the designer can make the image we want to observe more clear. With a creative impulse, the designer can use this to create secondary objects out of the negative space, exploiting a reversal in the figure/ground relation-ship. Graphic designer M.C. Escher is a good example of someone who experimented with this process to great success. More directly, many logo designers have seen fit to use this space to their advantage, like the "arrow" between the "e" and "x" in the FedEx logo. It is one of the most important lessons to learn in design, that the space between forms is just as important as the forms themselves. **JF**

Thou shall not make everything on a page the same size

Commentary Good composition is a mix of scale, shape, and color working together dynamically with harmony. A good trick to create dynamic composition is to think of the page or screen, not as a flat surface, but as a window into a three-dimensional world. The closer an object is to the viewer, the larger it will be. The more distant objects will be smaller. If all objects are the same size, they will appear to be static on a flat surface. Creating multiple sizes creates a dynamic and unexpected composition. Unless the goal is to bore the viewer, the scale must not simply be slightly different, but have extreme scale changes from tiny to huge. Combine giant type with small lines of text. Mix a small set of images with a large one. Use an extreme close-up of a face with a distant background. **SA**

152

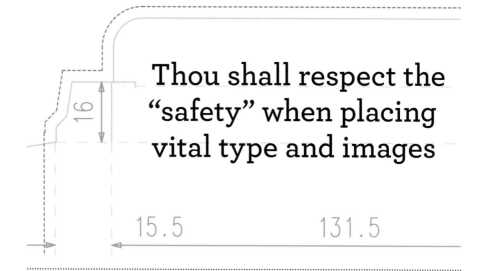

Thou shall respect the "safety" when placing vital type and images

Commentary When your parents told you not to play in the road, it wasn't so that they could boss you around and show you that they were in control and send you hurtling toward decades of therapy and low self-esteem (well, not in my family, at least). It was because they knew that if you were busy picking up jacks or drawing on the pavement in chalk, eventually an 18-wheeler would come along and make a kid-shaped pancake out of you. And while they might have gotten out of paying your college tuition, they didn't have a spatula big enough to pry you off the interstate AND they actually cared about your well-being. The same is true of the kind folks that make up your production templates. The safety is there for a reason, because, if you flirt with it often enough, the production process will eventually burn you and trim away vital copy and images. Respect the invisible line. It's for your own good. **JF**

Thou shall not silhouette and drop shadow every last image

Commentary The computer allows designers to create forms previously extremely difficult to do. Twenty years ago, hand cut film made a silhouetted image, and a photographer created drop shadows with light and film. Today, the magic wand can help create a silhouette in moments. And a drop shadow is created with a Photoshop® effect. This may seem like a modern miracle, in the same league as antibiotics and cell phones. But it is not. This is another instance of the saying,

"Just because one can do something, doesn't mean one should do something." Creating a silhouette is the appropriate solution at times. Adding a drop shadow digitally may also be necessary in limited situations. Like eating French pastries, these things should be done in moderation. Too many images with silhouettes and drop shadows make a project look like an ad for a stock image company. At best this is clean and simple. At worst, this solution is dull, dull, dull, expected, and trite. **SA**

154

Thou shall return to the creative brief numerous times during the creative process

Commentary I cannot stress enough how important a creative brief is to a project. It doesn't have to be extensive or too involved. Actually, I prefer that it be simple and short. It is a brief, after all. Take the time to talk through your project with your client and establish their priorities, and then rank them in the order of importance. The focus should always be on the top two or three on your list, with anything to follow a bonus if it can be done. When you both agree that you have a list that applies to the project at hand, type it up and share it, and agree that you both will keep it close. If you refer to it often when designing, you will surely help them accomplish their goals. On the client side, referring to the brief takes away a lot of the subjectivity and keeps everyone focused on what is best for the project. A win-win. **JF**

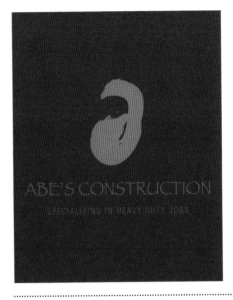

Thou shall not project a personal style at the expense of the client

Commentary Every city has a design firm that becomes sort of famous for the wrong reasons. It is not because they are helping clients reach unexpected success, or financial windfalls, or helping change the world for the better—it is because they have a recognizable style. They use the same layouts and fonts whether they are selling swimsuits or condos, saving the seals, or filling seats at the theater. It is depressing because it is unfounded attention—but it is generally short lived once the clients realize that not only do their materials look like everything else that the firm designs, but they have been left in a precarious position where competitors can swipe their branding just by using the same colors and fonts, etc. Style can be a quick fix, but true solutions that provide value to all involved require a great deal more work. We all use our tools in certain ways, and prospective clients should be able to see how we problem-solve for others, while knowing that we will give them a final result that can only be unique to them. **JF**

156

Thou shall understand designing "above the fold" in both print and online

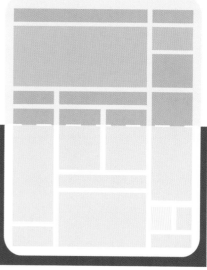

Commentary Designing a layout on your screen is a far cry from how it will ultimately be used, whether it is a publication or a website. You have the ability to zoom in and out, controlling your perspective and usually keeping it at a size and determination where it looks best to you. You might revel in a tiny detail at the bottom of a magazine cover, or your ability to find room for some fund-raising information toward the lower right on a website front page. Thinking it's a job well done, you will be quickly disappointed when you go to the grocery store only to see the racks covering up your beautiful work, or looking over the shoulder of your better half as they click past the website before ever scrolling down. Respect the fold and you won't pay that dire price. The term comes from newspaper layout, when the portion you would see in the racks and at your doorstep was the front of the folded final copy, so everything that was determined to be vital had to be "above the fold," lest it be missed. **JF**

APPROVED

Thou shall know a good design in one's gut

Commentary We may all share a communication with the spirit world, have a sixth sense, or simply intuit well. Whatever the reason, we all have a "gut instinct." At times, this instinct tells us to slow down at an intersection, or pause before we scream at the postal service employee. This instinct also usually tells a designer that he or she has the right solution. It's the idea the designer had and then sketched on a napkin while meeting with the client. Or, the solution he or she keeps returning to when walking home at night. It's a good practice to explore many ideas and concepts. This should be done without editing oneself; one bad idea may lead to a great one. But, the right idea will always feel right. Some designers believe work must be hard. They believe that the only good ideas come from endless hours of suffering and difficult labor. Design does not need to be hard and over-wrought. A simple and smart idea that feels good may be exactly correct. **SA**

158

Thou shall understand how visual "closure" works

Commentary At some point in our lives we have been confronted with someone wanting to show us a visual trick that involves seeing a pattern. Then we are shocked to scan further to the side and see that a red dot is in the middle of it or that no red dot exists in a pattern, or any number of tricks on our mind. We can all agree on one thing: these things are annoying, and so are the people that present them to us. However, they play on a very important visual practice: our ability to visualize the remainder of an image when we are given incomplete information, which is referred to as visual "closure." We use this so that we can process and understand things quickly without bogging down in every last detail. Glance quickly at the circles above for a quick demonstration. As designers, we can use this to our advantage, as well as be conscious of it so that vital information is not lost to the viewer. The eye is in the detail, even if some of the detail is left out on purpose. **JF**

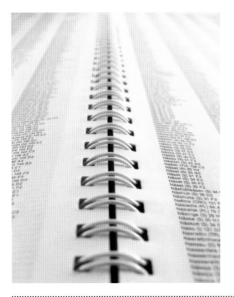

Thou shall learn how to format an index correctly

Commentary On paper an index would seem to be the simplest thing in the world to get right, but typesetting the perfect index requires practice. You need to understand how the various levels of indent work for entries that run to two or more lines. Two levels of indent are sufficient for most indexes, where you have subentries to main topics which run to a subsequent second line. If any one entry runs over to a third line the indent should remain the same until the next unique entry begins. Try to avoid anything more complex than this in terms of indexing levels. A well designed index should be easy to navigate. Liberal use of another font weight, perhaps for the page numbers, can help to improve the look as well as ease of use. Indexes are usually the last thing that gets done before repro and print, but don't scrimp on the time and effort you put in, as theoretically those pages could be the most used pages in the whole publication. **TS**

Color

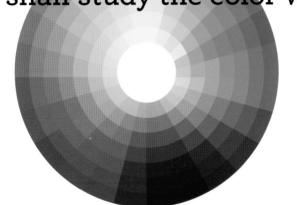

Thou shall study the color wheel

Commentary The study of color and how it's used revolves around the simple concept of color wheels, which help to explain visually how color is created from either light (RGB) or pigment (CMYK), and how the relationship between different colors comes about. We normally represent a color wheel as, surprise, a circle with distinct segments progressing through 360 degrees. Alternatively they're shown as gradated tints of merging color, familiar to everyone as the color picker incorporated into many applications, where color is more saturated at the outside edge. It's sometimes also shown as a strip, as in the color picker in Photoshop. The important thing to note is how a color wheel is structured: red, yellow, and blue—the *primary* colors—form the three main spokes of the wheel. These colors are blended to form *secondary* colors: orange, green, and violet. Blending primary and secondary colors produces *tertiary* colors, and so on. Complementary colors are those that sit directly opposite one another on a color wheel, for example primary blue and secondary orange. **TS**

161

Thou shall learn about hue, saturation, and value

H

S

V

Commentary Hue (another name for color), saturation, and value (or brightness) are the three components which combine to form the multitude of colors we see around us every day. Saturated colors are strong or vivid; desaturated colors are grayer and can be mixed by adding either black or white pigment (or more or less light) to pure hues such as the primary colors. Value is the measure of how dark or light a hue appears compared to black or white. It all sounds a bit scientific unless you try to simplify it, so try squinting at a standard color wheel.

You'll notice that the brighter colors like yellow stay brighter because they already have a higher value relative to black compared to, say, dark violet. Another good way to illustrate this is with the color picker on a Mac. Saturation is 0 percent (or white) at the center of the wheel and 100 percent at the outside edge. The slider to the right controls the value with 100 percent brightness at the top and 0 percent (totally dark) at the bottom. **TS**

Thou shall understand the difference between additive and subtractive mixing

Commentary This is simpler to explain than some of the other areas of color theory. Additive mixing is all about light and subtractive mixing is all about pigments. When you look at your computer screen, all the colors you see are the result of additive mixing where red, green, and blue light combine. Mixing all three colors together produces white light, adding green and blue make magenta, adding green and red make yellow, and adding red and blue make cyan. This is additive mixing. Subtractive mixing happens when printed pigments absorb particular wavelengths of light—what we see on a printed page is actually the reflected light that hasn't been absorbed by the pigment. This is why we use cyan, magenta, and yellow pigments for process printing—they're the colors produced by the additive color model so work in reverse when printed. Black is added into the mix for four-color process printing to produce a purer black than that achieved by mixing solid cyan, magenta, and yellow together, and it also provides better control over value (or brightness). **TS**

163

Thou shall understand the function of different color models

Commentary Color models can also be referred to as color spaces and are all important when it comes to maintaining color consistency in a workflow when combined with color profiles. They're all about mathematics but don't worry, you don't actually have to do the math yourself. The models that most designers will recognize are RGB and CMYK. These are *device-dependent* models, meaning they're designed to facilitate color reproduction on devices such as monitors and printing systems. They also have a limited color range—known as a color gamut (which you can read about in Rule #165), so some colors produced with these models aren't always true to the original, but are governed by whatever device you're looking at or printing with. *Device-independent* models, on the other hand, mimic the way our eyes perceive color so are technically more accurate to the original. LAB is the most common model of this type and has a much larger color gamut than other models. It's popular with designers that do a lot of color correction because it can separate an image's luminance (or brightness) from its color. **TS**

Thou shall ensure your color settings remain synchronized across all applications

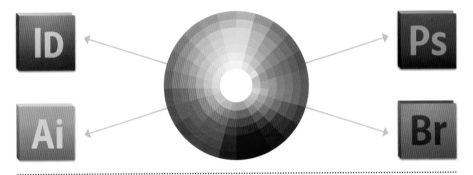

Commentary One of the great advantages to using an integrated suite of design tools is the fact that you can create similar (or similarish, at least) working environments when switching from one to another. The Adobe® Creative Suite® is particularly good at this and pays special attention to the synchronization of color settings for different color models or working spaces through a centralized function in Adobe® Bridge. It also allows the user to synchronize how applications treat images as they move from, say, Photoshop® to InDesign® or Illustrator®.

Why is this important? Well, it's unlikely that you'll be using Photoshop® to design a layout or InDesign® to create a complex vector illustration, and if you can't rely on consistent color when moving between applications there's really no point in paying any attention to the colors you choose to specify, as your final results won't be predictable or consistent. It's not a creative process as such, but color consistency is extremely important if you want to see color proofs and final output that's a close match to what you've been looking at on your computer screen. **TS**

165

Thou shall not ignore the constraints of color gamuts

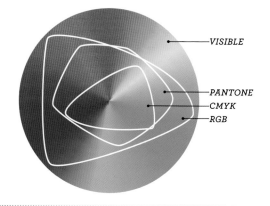

VISIBLE

PANTONE
CMYK
RGB

Commentary Did you ever wonder why you can create an amazingly vibrant red onscreen but can't seem to get it to print out with the same kind of intensity of color? The reason it's not possible to translate certain colors from screen to paper has a lot to do with color gamuts. A color gamut represents the complete range of colors that any one color model is capable of producing in print. It also represents the complete range of colors that a device can capture, as with a camera or scanner, or a display, as with a computer screen. Screens use the RGB model to display color, and an RGB gamut is larger than the CMYK gamut used for four-color printing. This is why you can't print that amazing red with CMYK—it's outside the CMYK color gamut. Spot colors like Pantones are not dependent on the CMYK color gamut as they're mixed from pigments, so a much brighter red can be achieved if printed as a spot color. This is true of many colors limited by a CMYK gamut. **TS**

Thou shall get to grips with color rendering intents

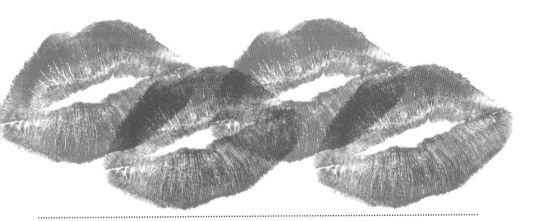

Commentary Rendering intents help to address the issue of the RGB gamut being larger than the CMYK gamut by controlling what happens when colors are converted from RGB to CMYK. There are four rendering intents to choose from and each produces a subtly different result, which may or may not suit a project's needs. *Perceptual* attempts to preserve colors by compressing them into the CMYK gamut, so tends to alter most colors and can reduce saturation. *Saturation* keeps colors that can be produced using CMYK but changes out of gamut colors while attempting to also preserve saturation. This can cause significant color shifts so isn't great for color critical imagery. *Absolute Colorimetric* keeps colors within the CMYK gamut intact and converts out of gamut colors to the closest possible hue at the expense of a little saturation, but can produce a slight color cast in white areas. *Relative Colorimetric* is the default for most uses as it's similar to Absolute Colorimetric but also adjusts the white point, thus reducing color casts. If in doubt, always go for Relative Colorimetric. **TS**

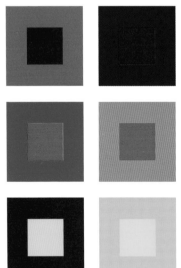

Thou shall not neglect the fact that colors change according to their surroundings

Commentary Color is subjective and emotional. It is challenging to convince someone to like pink if they were repeatedly locked in a pink closet as a child. This makes color one of the most problematic elements designers use. Added to the subjective nature of color is the way we see color. First, we all experience color in our own way. Warm red will appear different to every person viewing it. To one person it looks orange, to another red. It is vital to be accommodating when dealing with color. Telling someone they are wrong about a color choice is to tell them they are a bad person. If these hurdles were not high enough, color changes according to its environment. What seems to be a soft yellow in the designer's office can be an awful yellow-green under the client's fluorescent light. The primary colors, red, blue, and yellow, are the most consistent in different surroundings. Complex colors, such as violet are more volatile and easily shift from blue to purple. When showing color options to a client, it is best to explain that color changes in different settings. **SA**

Thou shall look at what surrounds us for color inspiration

Commentary A common obstacle for designers is choosing colors. The swatch panel of default colors in Adobe® Illustrator® exists for broad gestures of color. It is not a color palette. It is, like the default shapes in Illustrator®, ordinary and overdone. A strong color palette is as important as the typeface choices. A good color palette will be unique, seductive, and harmonious. The natural world is a good place to look for inspiration. A poplar tree is not green. It is a mix of blue green, lime green, sliver green, light brown, cool gray, and white. The sunset is not red. It is dark blue, light blue, pink, orange, and yellow. A smart process to create a color palette is to take an image of a natural setting and sample distinct colors from different parts. The result will be a system of colors ranging from light to dark, and intense to soft. But they will always remain in harmony and be unique to your experience. **SA**

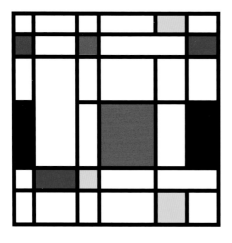

Thou shall draw color inspiration from great works of art

Commentary If you're looking for a new colorway for your latest project, there are lots of very useful resources out there in print and online where thousands of different color combinations or schemes can be referenced and compared. However, there's another way of looking for color combinations that will not only provide a real-world view of how colors might combine but has been provided by the absolute experts of color. Look at art. People have been experimenting with color combinations for thousands of years and it's all out there for us to look at. You can even gear your choice of art to the kind of project you're working on. If you want an earthy combination of blacks and browns take a look at some cave paintings. If you want rich and luxurious colors try something by Hans Holbein the Younger. For bold bright combinations try Vincent van Gogh, or some of Mark Rothko's work. If you're not so much into painting but like more graphic work, look at Lichtenstein, Mondrian, or Warhol. The colors are all there for the taking. **TS**

Thou shall not use beige to attract attention

Commentary Attracting attention requires volume. This is true audibly. When you want a friend across the street to see you, you shout, "Hey, Dick! Over here." This is true physically. Slamming a freshman against a locker will get their attention. And it is true visually. Stop signs are red and have large type. Beige is not loud. Beige, gray, and tan may be sophisticated and classic, but they are not good when competing for attention. Beige is like a silent killer. It will slowly creep into a project. The image may feel too bright, so it is desaturated. The type color seems too bold, so it is softened. The final result is an overall beige tone. Online as a website it is beige-green on some monitors and looks boring. As a poster it hangs unnoticed by passers-by. Do not fear color; do not retreat to the safe, quiet, and deadly world of beige. **SA**

171

Thou shall remember that colored type can provide as much emphasis as bolding

AUDACES FORTUNA IUVAT

Commentary There are easy and obvious pathways to creating emphasis for a bit of type in your layout. That doesn't necessarily mean that they are always the best avenue to accomplish that, though. Much in the way that a highway can provide the quickest trip to your destination, it can also dull your senses to the trip itself, and when used too often, become clogged and slow and a worse option than doing nothing at all. The simple bold may be your reactive selection when trying to highlight a word or section, but take time to consider color as well. Using a color to bring out a repeated phrase or word can be hypnotic; using a slash of red to create terror over a phrase can add tension. There are so many powerful tools at your disposal; with just the tiny click of adding a wash of color you can forever change the viewer's perception. **JF**

Thou shall think of white space as a color and use it positively

Commentary I find the employment of white space in any design is a crucial factor to the design's success and its usage should be a consideration from the outset. I'm not just talking margins here but factoring in white as a part of the layout so that the elements of the page are separated, framed, and supported. In addition, the positioning and control of white space will lead the reader through the design, subtly being taken by the hand through the content.

When working on books with predominantly photographic content, rather than design the layout with the picture's format as the priority, I think about how the white space can work with each *specific* picture so it can be presented at its best. Try experimenting with different layouts, using a single image—you will be surprised the extent to which white space can alter the mood, pacing, and presentation of the content. **PD**

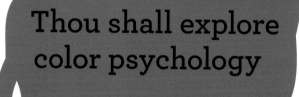

Thou shall explore color psychology

Commentary Psychology generates skepticism among nonsubscribers, but it's not all (ahem) bull. A bull doesn't chase a cape because it's red—in fact bulls are color blind. He does it because the matador is waving it in his face and because he doesn't like the matador very much. Seriously though, color can be used by designers to invoke a range of emotions and behaviors. Red is particularly interesting, coming from the warm area of the spectrum, and conjures feelings of warmth and comfort as well as anger, hostility,

and danger. Colors from the cool end, such as blues and greens, can be used to call forth a sense of calm, but can also create feelings of sadness or indifference. It's well worth reading up a little on how the psychology of color works as it'll help to inform your choice of colors for your design projects, adding some context to those choices, which in turn will supply you with some ammunition to fire back at your client when they utter the immortal line, "I can see what you're saying, but I don't like blue." **TS**

Thou shall not follow the rules of color psychology slavishly

Commentary There are many rules and theories about color. Psychologically, orange is agitating. Blue is calming. Red is exciting. Pink is restful. Like all rules, however, following them slavishly results in solutions that are expected and rigid. These rules change. At one time, eating steak was considered healthy. Now, we are told, it is not healthy. In a month, it may be healthy again. Orange was used in fast food restaurants to create agitation and keep the customer from lingering. Now orange is seen as hip and exciting. It was a cardinal sin to use red for financial institutions, as it signified the bank being "in-the-red." Today this rule no longer applies. Knowing the rules is valuable. Then throw them out and use what is appropriate for communication and visual interest. **SA**

175

Thou shall remember that colors mean different things in different cultures

Commentary You have spent months perfecting a new brand of perfume that has a name inspired by royalty. Tweaking your glistening crown logo and your type solution filled with flourishes, soon gives way to the packaging design. A lush purple finds itself gripping all aspects of the brand. It feels important, and expensive, while still being romantic and sexy. The line launches to great acclaim, except in Thailand, where the distributor can't even find many outlets willing to give it a chance. Splintering your Asian revenues, the corporate folks can't believe they are only now learning that Thailand considers purple a color of mourning and one worn by its widows. It is an important consideration to take in when working on projects with international applications and appeal. Yellow is a color of courage in Japan, yet often linked to cowardice in the United States, and burdened with the same albatross of mourning that purple carries in Thailand, when used in Egypt. It's so easy to use a color, but much more difficult (and valuable) to understand its significance. **JF**

Thou shall choose colors for a reason rather than simply because you like the color

Commentary In a lot of ways, this is one of the most difficult rules to abide by, and a sign that you have finally given yourself over 100 percent to being the best possible designer that you can be—for your client. We all have favorite colors, and we all have many that we avert our eyes from when encountered in real life. As much as we learn to appreciate that a scripty font is not going to work for a monster truck rally, we need to grasp that our favorite colors are rarely the perfect ones to drape on our client's business. While it seems obvious that a branding for an ice company involve blues in some capacity, it should also be just as obvious that they be cool blues, regardless of whether you tend to prefer purple-infused deeper blues. Always have a reason for selecting every element in your design, right down to the all-important color. **JF**

Thou shall not be afraid to be bold with your color choices

Commentary A common insult used by eight-year-old boys is, "You're a wimp." Nobody wants to be a wimp. Most people in the world want to feel important and strong. Design can reinforce a sense of strength and confidence. Bold color choice is one tactic used to communicate power. This is not an endorsement to use fluorescent pink on every project. Bold color can be a relentless palette of pastel colors, or a rich combination of dark gray tones. It can also be extremely bright or unexpected combinations. Mix avocado green and bright orange, or brown and pink. As long as it is purposeful and handled with courage it will be right. Wimpy color choices include the expected combinations such as flat navy blue and medium gray. These colors are appropriate for outfits on a college or job interview, or meeting grandparents for lunch. They may be appropriate for an extraordinarily stodgy insurance firm. They do not, however, say, "We are the s%#@," in design. **SA**

Thou shall remember that people like bright things—brown is not exciting

Commentary If a baby lying in a crib is presented with two mobiles, one in bright colors, the other in browns, he or she will always grab for the bright one. As people age, this doesn't change. As designers, we are told repeatedly that the unpleasant tones are the fashionable colors. Baby-poop green, brown, and dingy yellow are supposedly sophisticated. But when a designer presents a packaging solution with these and the client resists, the designer claims, "They just don't understand good design." This is not true. The client is not required to understand "good design." The client should understand his or her own business, the audience, and communication goals. No client has ever said, "Please design something that will repulse people and make my business fail." The client is responding the way 95 percent of the intended audience will. People, from birth until death, will always gravitate toward the bright colors. **SA**

179

Thou shall learn how the transparency of a color or ink affects those it overlaps

Commentary One of the true glories of the silkscreen explosion of the past decade is that it exposes more and more designers to the joys of overprinting. As process color has become increasing affordable, trying to do so with spot colors on an offset job via overprinting, duotones, and other tricks seems to be going by the wayside. But you should never forget that you always have more colors on hand than the cans of ink bought for the job would indicate. Watching inks printed over the top of one another, whether it is Bradbury Thompson's famous CMYK experiments, or your current favorite gig-poster artist, allows us to see how the inks change one another and create a multitude of effects. From the straightforward third color that comes from making a green by printing a blue over a yellow, we can see a totally different effect by printing a darker gray over the same yellow, yielding a subtle shift to a deeper gray in those areas. Oh, the possibilities! **JF**

000% Cyan 010% Magenta 100% Yellow 000% Black	
000% Cyan 100% Magenta 080% Yellow 004% Black	
100% Cyan 045% Magenta 000% Yellow 000% Black	
080% Cyan 000% Magenta 090% Yellow 000% Black	
000% Cyan 060% Magenta 095% Yellow 000% Black	
100% Cyan 000% Maganta 030% Yellow 005% Black	

Thou shall not use Pantone spot colors in a four-color print job

Commentary If I had a dollar for every commissioned layout I've ever had to prepress which had a rogue Pantone color hiding away within its pages, I would have enough for a good night out on the town at the very least. The use of Pantone, or spot, colors in a project destined for four-color printing is disastrous for a number of reasons. Firstly, a spot color must print as an extra fifth color which adds to your print bill, so it will mess up your quote and could cost you dearly. Secondly, the vast majority of Pantone colors can't be reproduced accurately from the four process colors, cyan, magenta, yellow, and black, even if your software forces them to separate out. The problem lies in the fact that a Pantone book is often the only resource designers have at their disposal when choosing colors, so they make color choices which in reality will never be achieved within the constraints of four-color printing. If you know your project must print only in four colors, put your Pantone book in a drawer and resist the temptation to take a peek at all costs. **TS**

Thou shall not use more than two Pantone colors with a CMYK print job

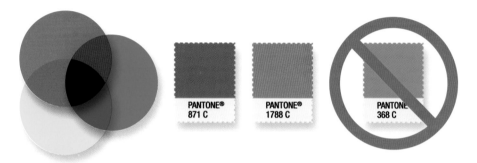

PANTONE®
871 C

PANTONE®
1788 C

PANTONE
368 C

Commentary There's an obvious benefit to using the CMYK printing process—you can create any color you want by mixing the four inks. To have *more* than two Pantone colors as well would be superfluous. It may be that you are running a fluorescent or a metallic ink (or both) with the CMYK set, which is fine, although you should always make an effort to show constraint, otherwise your end design could be quite vulgar and "showy" when printed. Another reason is the cost.

There are five-, six-, seven-, and even eight-color presses, although most commonly found is six. So that's six inks: four taken up by CMYK, then two more inks or, more commonly, one special ink and a varnish to finish, allowing the print job to be done in a single pass. To add more special colors would mean running the sheets through the press again, which would be expensive and wasteful. Also, you have to ask yourself: would your design really be any better? **PD**

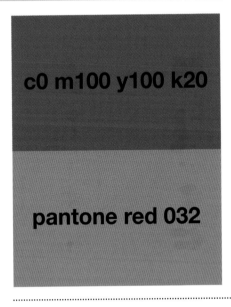

c0 m100 y100 k20

pantone red 032

Thou shall use process color-built reds with no Pantone selected

Commentary In the village of Pantonia, behind the rainbow-swirled gates, lies a magical factory of Wonkaesque wizardry. It is here that they manage to create 40 new colors each year, seemingly out of thin air. Plucking a toucan feather yields a decade's worth of hip and inspirational shades. Their dedication to putting a code number on every blip of intensity that our eye registers over a lifetime is admirable, to say the least. Much like the average closet at an ad agency, they even have multiple versions of a simple black. So why is it that they have never been able to create a decent red? It's a sad fact that, no matter how many batches those oompa loompas swirl back at the plant, they just can't get it right. It's a shame, as red is often called into service in our world. Thank goodness we can start at 0/100/100/20 and go from there. **JF**

Thou shall not specify print colors with RGB values

Commentary I know it's a real blow whenever we have to face this sad fact, but you can't print RGB colors. RGB colors are made from projected light; CMYK and Pantone colors are made from pigments which generate reflected light. RGB colors are generally brighter and more saturated because the RGB color gamut is much larger than the CMYK equivalent. It's tempting to look at a bright red RGB color on your computer screen and think how great it would look flooding the front cover of the brochure you're working on, but I'm afraid it isn't

going to happen. It's simply not possible to achieve with the four-color process, although some Pantones can get close because white pigment can be mixed in. So if the budget allows for extra spot colors, that's the way to go. It's even more important to bear this in mind now that work is increasingly presented on a laptop or iPad screen, so please try to explain to your client why the finished job won't look quite the same before they take delivery. **TS**

Thou shall not create tints from tints

100%
45%

Commentary So you have a layout all set to go and a colleague wanders over to ask you what CMYK percentages you've used to create that really cool blue-green background tint. You happily take a look while congratulating your colleague on his excellent appraisal of your color choices, only to find that it's a 45 percent tint of 75 percent cyan and 30 percent yellow which is, umm, hang on while I get a calculator. You see, really annoying isn't it? It's not a disaster as such because the color will still look good in the final job, but it's not great not knowing what the color actually is. The point I'm making is, by all means create percentage tints from spot colors, but not from colors that are already percentage tints. There is a quick, calculator-free fix. Select the color and delete it from the Swatches panel, replacing it with an unnamed swatch, then add unnamed swatches back in. Your actual color will reveal itself to be 34 percent cyan and 14 percent yellow. Nice! **TS**

185

Thou shall not screen a color to less than 7 percent and expect to see it on the printed page

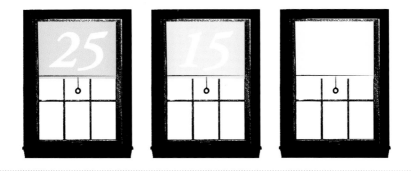

Commentary You know what looks dazzling in its subtlety on your computer screen? A 5 percent screen of your spot color. You know what has nary a chance of showing up on the printed page? A 5 percent screen of your spot color. The thing about commercial printing is that there can easily be a variation in how heavy the ink is running. Combined with the gain, or lack thereof, on varying sheets of paper, it is wise to keep a 10 percent variation in the back of your mind. That is a worst-case scenario, but using newsprint or similar sheets can easily see it come to fruition. The reason? Using such a small number of dots, which is what happens when it is such a light shade, gives the printer little leeway. If you really desire such a light color, selecting a Pantone that is that color at 100 percent is the way to go. **JF**

Thou shall not use process color for small body text

Nihictur, ut quod unditas quibust doluptam doluptur aut ut od quis enimost autet as sam sum id explia quis in cor am dolut ut aria vollupt ionest, vendest, occat es quatur sum res incti ut volleni magnistio. Ut pa peritae comminus enet quiaspe ditaque prorecum velecte ndanisi qui rercienda in rempor aut que nam fugiam quo ma cusa dolut laborepta inctescid quam doluptae. Onsequiae nam volorro ribusam qui odit qui aut poreic te dolupta doluptas molo od ullupta sit re nos re, nonsedipsum ent et vendam sitio. Nam, quist maior auditis sitiatquia quis eum esto est a velectur rehendi blabo. Itatius sim eturem. Volecti oriatur? Quis veribus ditaspelecae prat.

Nes eum ratibus, officto riorios ide porem acest, sum enderi recum ut post quam quo quibus in nobis estis mod mi, temporest, officip idictus sim idessit atibust es reprepero cusaperum aut untur, optas poreper iorposseque late nobist aut estium aut volora dolupta tiunto bearum quam que in et untiaerro doluptam quodit asimpedi aut autasim que inctur remos volorep erferum as venita ni comnis

Commentary Process colors—cyan, magenta, yellow, and black—combine to create four-color images. Black is a good choice for small body text, as it is legible and prints clearly. Cyan, yellow, and magenta do not work for small body text. First, returning to how we read, we look at individual letters and combine them to make words, which make sentences, and paragraphs. Differentiating the characters is the basis of the process. Cyan, yellow, and magenta are too intense to work well together. Alone, they are each too intense or light to be seen clearly. Secondly, a paragraph printed in magenta is bright and tiring to read. It's as if you ask the viewer to look at the sun. It looks nice, but you will go blind when you stare at it too long. To be safe, make sure text is legible. Body text should be set in darker tones or black. **SA**

Thou shall learn how colors can share tonal qualities

Commentary In its simplest terms, color tone is created by adding gray to a pure hue. Knowing this, you can see that adding the same amount of gray to varying colors would create the same tonal qualities. However, you are unlikely to be standing by as the process of adding them in is completed. The Pantone books can be helpful, as they can show a tonal range in sequential colors at times. More importantly, they provide color chips so that you can match up options and train your eye as to whether they share tonal qualities. Why is this important? At a base level, the eye requires contrast to process information, so even though you have placed a green next to an orange, if they are the same tone, they ultimately blend together into one shape. This can be a desired effect, but one that can only be properly achieved by understanding how it occurs. **JF**

188

Thou shall learn how to group colors into hot and cold groups

Commentary When starting out on a project, I often try to think about the colors in the most basic sense possible; should they be hot or cold? There are numerous reasons for choosing a different palette, and many projects will require a combination of hot and cold colors, while others benefit immensely from being cohesive. Many people will make the mistake of quickly lumping basic colors into each side, with no leeway available. The proliferation of color options has allowed for a greater breadth. Blues, inherently in the cool category, can take on doses of magenta until they find themselves in the hot group, where most purples will reside. Blazing hot yellows will give way to cooler light greens. Even grays themselves have been lumped into cool and warm sections by Pantone. It is a distinction that can often give your color selections a needed collective feeling, and also create impactful decisions when only one hot or cold color is injected into the solution. **JF**

189

Thou shall use value contrast to divert or draw the viewer's attention

Commentary Fear can be quite useful at times. When facing an oncoming train, lion on safari, or angry ruffian, fear is a wonderful tool. Fear is not good in design. When the designer is frightened that the solution is too aggressive, bold, or exciting, he or she may fall into the trap of mildness. It begins by saying, "Perhaps the colors are too strong." Then the shapes all become a similar scale. And finally, the black tones are changed to mid-range gray. The result is a mild, pointless, and bland solution. Contrast is your friend. Strong value changes in contrast attract attention. They stand out in a crowded visual environment. At the extreme of value contrast are 100% black and pure white. And they work. The world is saturated with multiple mid-tone colors, creating an overall low contrast impression. Strong black and white tones may seem "old-fashioned," but this combination is rarely used. In the midst of a plethora of four-color images advertising products on billboards, imagine the impression of a simple black and white, high contrast solution. **SA**

Thou shall learn to love the Eyedropper tool

Commentary I've been using Adobe InDesign since Version 2 but it took me a long time to realize how useful the Eyedropper tool is. I thought it simply stored the color of any object you click on, enabling you to fill another object or apply the same color to text, like it does in Adobe® Photoshop®. How wrong I was—you can copy type attributes, too. Click on an item of text, even some text in another document, then drag over another item of text with the Eyedropper, and bingo, it copies not just the color of the text but many additional stored attributes to the new selection. While it's true that good practice dictates the use of style sheets for all text formatting, especially in long documents, there's always a use for this functionality when you're working on a one-off job like a poster or flyer, or when you're experimenting with type styles prior to applying style sheets. Time to stop ignoring the Eyedropper tool, I think. **TS**

Thou shall use color to create movement

Commentary The ability to create movement using color is actually fairly easy, creating the illusion of action. When an image, or sequence of colors, has a wide variation in value running throughout it (note that this is very different from a layout that pans across to build to a different value), it jumps about to the viewer's eye, allowing for a kinetic reaction. Once you have this knowledge, you can harness it to create busy jumbles that literally dance in front of the viewer, or pull back and create a soothing effect with colors of the same value taking over. If you are feeling particularly bold, you can create color sequences, where the same color repeats in a pattern, creating a rhythmic quality. This also allows you to appreciate painting, where this can be seen to its fullest effect, from the high contrast rhythm of a Mondrian to the energetic sky of a Van Gogh, which separates his simple scenes from the rest. **JF**

Thou shall use color to create tension

Commentary Explaining visual tension is like trying to describe yellow to someone. It is an aspect of composition that uses unexpected color, shape, or scale to create energy. Often, designers create tension in their work, not to invoke anxiety, but to give the viewer a more dynamic experience. Using dissimilar, or jarring color combinations is one way to do this. Understanding the spatial properties of color is another way. For example, warm tones appear to advance in three-dimensional space, and cool tones recede. If a large object appears closer to the viewer, and smaller objects are more distant, then it would be logical for the large object to use a color such as red. If you reverse the expected here, and make the closer, larger object the cool color, and the distant/smaller object red, tension is created. The viewer is being told two opposing ideas. Color can be used to create tension by combining tones that vibrate, such as blue and red. Using color in unexpected ways, such as a blue chicken, or Tower Bridge in pink, can also create tension. **SA**

193

Thou shall use color to create calm

Commentary While recessive and banal should never be the goal of a project, a calm tone can be required. Frightening subjects such as urological surgery, dental work, and airplane safety require colors that are calming and reassuring. The first step is to understand the audience and their concerns. Does the audience need comforting, to feel safe, or put at ease? If so, calm colors can achieve this. Calm colors do not need to be uniformly light pastel tones. The context of each assignment dictates the color choices. Blood red is a bad choice for surgical brochures and websites. However, red may be perfect as a signage choice in a complex environment. While there are exceptions, calming colors are less vibrant. They contain a higher percentage of white or black than a pure primary tone. Yellow can be made calming by adding white. A soft butter yellow isn't as jarring and aggressive as primary yellow, but still communicates optimism. **SA**

194

Thou shall not place analogous colors next to each other

Commentary Well, we were bound to end up in color theory class at some point, eh? Analogous colors are those that appear next to one another on the color wheel. Included in an overall palette, they can create a sense of harmony in your solution. Should you place them next to one another, however, they bask in their similarity and blend together in the worst possible way. Where we learned earlier to play tricks with tonal quality, here you often end up with violet next to a red and little to distinguish them but a muddy mess. In dressing yourself, the only thing worse than not matching is wearing two colors that are almost the same color. Picture yourself in a red and orange outfit and you will quickly realize that you were better off going all the way with either color, but are in big trouble trying to wedge them together. **JF**

Thou shall not place high-intensity complementary colors next to each other

Commentary Unless the goal of a project is to annoy the viewer, it is a good rule of thumb to not recklessly slam vibrant primary colors together. Blue and red will create a visual vibration. Blue and yellow are good for nautical applications when visual clarity may be challenged, but may be overwhelming on personal stationery. Red and yellow are perfect for McDonald's, but lack the sophistication that may be necessary for a refined high-end Japanese restaurant. As in all decisions, being aware of the context, communication, and desired psychological reaction will dictate the color choices. Yes, there are instances when using all three primary colors together works. A preschool's identity may seem to be a good place to use primary colors, and a square, circle, and triangle. But then it will match every other preschool logo from Toledo to Taipei. **SA**

Thou shall use fluorescent inks with a purpose

Commentary Fluorescent inks can add such a shine to a project, from the equivalent of an enormous glittering gold necklace swinging from your neck, to a crisp shoeshine on your patent leather loafers. They always make an impact. Using them in the proper manner can be the tougher part. Not every occasion is suited to flashy neckwear, though a snappy pair of loafers goes well with most everything. Using these types of ink brings an intense brilliance and you can add a spot color of fluorescent orange or green or yellow and instantly grab all of the available eyeballs, but it has to be appropriate and you should know that those looks are generally reserved for youthful entertainment and fashion-based applications. The more versatile option is adding it into your process inks to increase their intensity and shine. The ink comes into specialized use when the clear version is used on a project as a security measure, where it is only seen when exposed to UV light. **JF**

Thou shall utilize color profiles in your workflow

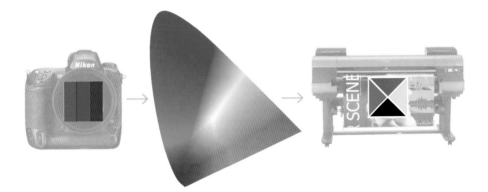

Commentary In order to manage and maintain the color of your artwork files, linked RGB images, and graphics, it's important to use color profiles and embed them into your work as you carry out any project. These profiles will then link to your color management system (CMS), which maintains color consistency as a project moves from the RGB environment of your computer display to the final CMYK print. At the beginning of any job, I always ask myself a number of questions: How are we printing this? What stock are we using? What is the color composition of the images? All these factors may have an impact on your choice of profile, which in turn plays an important part in maintaining the project's integrity and appearance. I often speak to the appointed printer and discuss the options available, and ask if they have profiles matched to their own presses which I could use. In doing this, I can then be sure that images embedded with the correct profile will display accurately on screen and the final print will be consistent with visuals. **PD**

Thou shall use "rich black" for large black backgrounds

Commentary Printing black over a small area, for example an uppercase X in 36pt Gill Sans Bold, will produce a strong impression with hard contrast between the black of the character and the white of the paper. However, if you print solid black over a large area, say the whole of a magazine spread, it won't look quite so solid. To make the black look *richer*, hence the term "rich black," you can underprint various percentages of the CMY colors to create "blacker blacks." A typical rich black uses a 50% tint of all three colors plus 100% black; but use a combination of 100% black with 70% cyan, 30% magenta, and 40% yellow for a "cool" black. If you need a warmer black try 100% black with 30% cyan, 60% magenta, and 60% yellow. Take care not to go too high with the percentages, however, as too much ink will produce too much wetness during printing. Always check with the printer to see what they recommend for their equipment. **TS**

Thou shall not allow rich black tints to exceed 300 percent ink coverage

Commentary Printing what is called "rich blacks"—the black printing with the three other inks (CMY)—can be troublesome when the percentage combination of all four colors adds up to more than 300 percent. All printers have a limit on their total area coverage (TAC), which refers to the maximum amount of ink allowed in the darkest areas of an image. The percentages vary from a maximum of around 300–340 percent for coated papers to 240–280 percent for uncoated papers. So to be on the safe side, I always check the values of any darker images (a night shot, for example) to ensure that the blacks of the sky and shadows don't exceed 300 percent. Not doing this makes the printing difficult to control when on press because of the huge amount of ink being laid down. It's also quite wasteful and too much ink will lead to "set-off" when drying, which means the image will be pressed onto the following sheet. A disastrous and very expensive issue to resolve and only fixed by going back and amending the guilty file, so check them first! **PD**

200

Thou shall take into account paper brightness and whiteness

Commentary Paper brightness has always been considered an important feature for any "white" printing stock, and shouldn't be confused with whiteness. *Brightness* is the percentage reflectance of blue light at a specific wavelength (457nm in fact) so is more quantifiable than *whiteness*, which is the percentage of light reflected at all wavelengths. The brightness of the pulps and pigments used in paper manufacture indicate how much whiteness can be achieved. Anyway—enough science, I think. High paper whiteness boosts the contrast of any printed area, so in turn can effectively increase the number of reproducible colors printed on the paper stock. It's not quite that simple, as colors will look different under different viewing conditions, but broadly speaking the color gamut of the color model used for printing will increase with the use of paper stock with a high whiteness. Conversely, paper with a slightly blue shade is considered whiter than stock which has a more neutral white shade and will make your colors really pop off the page. **TS**

Thou shall specify colors for packaging a little lighter than you want them to print

Commentary The very wise Robynne Raye of Modern Dog once bestowed upon me an invaluable piece of advice, pulling me aside and asking, "Have you ever seen a piece of packaging printed too light?" She then revealed that they often set the final files up a uniform 5 percent lighter than the versions proposed and approved, knowing that the gain on press will still likely leave them with a darker final product than expected. Decades into packaging assignments, I wish their observation wasn't true, but all you need to do is ask yourself if you have ever seen a package on a shelf and thought they held back a little on the ink for this one. Consumer items are often in a different sort of production cycle, sometimes printed with several other jobs, sometimes for other clients, or on insanely long print runs using rubber plates. This means different compromises need to be made at times, and trust me when I say that the pressperson will always add more ink to sort it out. **JF**

202

Thou shall never specify a color for print based on its on-screen appearance

Commentary This is an age-old problem that is still relevant today. When you look at colors on the screen, you see an "illuminated" representation of the color that is never entirely accurate. An electronic representation of a CMYK or Pantone color will not be the same as ink on paper. Although the two can get close on occasion, there will never be a perfect match. This has always caused difficulties for designers and for clients as what they see on their screen they believe will carry across and be printed. In addition, their screen will present differently than your screen, so already there is inconsistency. To guarantee the correct color is printed, I always use the color breakdowns or references supplied in the appropriate Pantone book and ensure the client sees them. Obtaining a proof will also ensure they understand how the colors will look for the end product. Be safe, never sorry. **PD**

Thou shall learn about underpainting

Commentary Some people understand underpainting. Everyone else doesn't know how to paint. I was a terrible student in my college painting class. I just didn't know it. Finally, my instructor tried to explain what was lacking in my work by insisting that I take a painting I had completed, and paint an entirely new piece over it. This stopped me from being precious about my work and also sent me on the most important color exploration of my life. Every single thing that I know about how colors interact with one another was informed by the experience. Midway through, she took the time to flesh out how underpainting works. Using only one paint color, I learned to make a monochromatic sketch on my canvas that added a uniform base and feeling for my final piece. I then learned how important layers of color could be— how yellow under the green grass was different from brown. It changed everything. **JF**

Thou shall ask your client color questions

Commentary After agonizing for weeks over a presentation to a huge nonprofit organization on their fundraising gala materials, I was stunned to hear, five minutes into the meeting, that none of my options were likely to work. My side of the room was still putting their jaws back in place when I notice the telltale look in the eyes of my main contacts sitting across from me. They could have told me this would happen. The reason was that the executive director's wife hated a certain color, one that was strewn throughout all of my options, and one that made conceptual sense. It was an extreme example, but I knew I had forgotten a vital step in my usual process. The time when I ask if there is anything I need to know about my client and colors. You should always ask in advance, but also be sure to ask following feedback. Can I never use green again? Or should I just shy away from that particular green? It will save you a lot of trouble. Trust me. **JF**

Thou shall respect an emotional response to a color from a client

Commentary One of the most frustrating things working in design can be when a client makes a subjective comment on color. Some of us, myself included, have set up presentation processes so that we can circumvent this as best as possible. However, it would be terribly naïve, and detrimental to your professional progress, to think that this will not occur time and time again. When your client says that they can't fathom using orange in their branding, because it was the color of their rival high school growing up, what do you do? If you think you are going to have any success forcing them to see the reasoning behind using that color, even if you are branding an orange juice company, you have already been told that you won't. When that emotional/irrational response happens, adjust, adapt, and most of all, respect it. You don't have to agree with it. But you are in your client's shoes, burdened by their color history. **JF**

Thou shall not get caught up in trendy colors for projects that need to stand the test of time

Commentary If you were dressing a person and knew that they had to wear the same clothes for 10, 20, 30 years or more, would you dress them in bell bottom jeans? Give them feathered Farah Fawcett hair, or better yet, a Mohawk? Pierce their nose or cover them in tattoos? Or would you research clothes until you had determined what was built to last, and what was trendy and sure to fall out of fashion soon enough? I hope that you would put in the time toward doing the research.

When you are doing the same on your design projects, creating a final product or brand that needs to hold its look far past the current time period, you should take even more care. Ignore those lists of what colors are "hot" and seem to be filled with made-up names for nonexistent fruits, and make solid decisions based on research and strategic thinking. **JF**

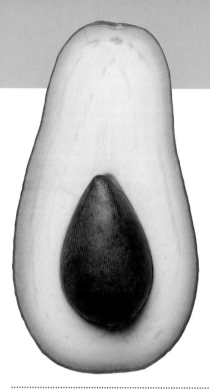

Thou shall remember that the popularity of certain colors shifts rapidly

Commentary Each year, multiple organizations publish lists of colors that will be in fashion the next year. One year, we are told that silver is the color that must be used if we are to remain relevant. The next year, brown is the new black. A designer must stay current with popular culture, taste, and attitudes. But, the designer should lead, not follow. When someone says, "That color is so dated," they are seeing it in a specific context. Avocado green will look dated on a 1970s refrigerator. Avocado green will appear fresh and current on an iPhone® cover. Coral will be dated on a 1955 Cadillac. It will be perfect on an identity for a forward-thinking nonprofit institution. The lesson is to create your own rules. If color is used with confidence in purposeful and bold ways, it will be appropriate and fresh. **SA**

Thou shall recognize that color palettes change depending on an audience's age

Commentary One of the most valued abilities in design and advertising is the ability to create for an audience well outside of your age group. The rabid pursuit of young consumers has made this talent, especially considering that kids can't enter the workplace to do this for themselves, a golden commodity. With the graying of our populations, an entirely new marketplace has opened up and marketing toward it has become a clear specialty. While many factors go into reaching these different groups, one factor that can often be forgotten is that age directly affects how the viewer reacts to color. One of the key factors is that children recognize a smaller range of colors, only responding to a widened palette as they grow older. Children also make early associations with specific colors (apples are red) and reward the use of bold and bright colors. As we become more savvy, or jaded, we also accept a wider range of colors and their applications. **JF**

Thou shall research the color palettes of your client's competitors

Commentary Strange things are revealed when a designer compiles a visual grouping of a client's competition. Typically, a clear language is uncovered. Part of this language is color. A similar palette for all of the competitors will be seen. For example, a search for financial institutions will disclose vast swaths of navy blue and forest green. The designer then has the choice to either ride the horse in the same direction, or go another way. A designer with little courage will look at the competitive research and determine that his or her client should look the same. The client may even say, "But everyone else uses blue." Conformity is valuable in the armed services. It is damaging in a competitive marketplace. The designer's job is to identify a client's strengths, weaknesses, competitors, and values. And then to create a visual solution that sets the client apart or above the competition. **SA**

Thou shall not let your personal color preferences hurt a project

Commentary Consider working on a book cover for a noted woman writer's new romantic novel. She has used carnation pink on each of her twelve other novels. Her bedroom is carnation pink, and her nickname is Pinky. Pink, however, makes you recoil. You consider it weak and a sign of women's oppression. What should you do? Clearly, using carnation pink is the correct choice. Trying to convince the author that your favorite colors, ocher and black, are better choices will have two effects. It will make the client angry, and you will be fired. More important, however, is that the ocher and black would damage Pinky's brand. The money and time spent to reinforce the identification of pink with Pinky will be discarded. Bluntly, pursuing your own personal color choice over the needs of the project will ruin lives. **SA**

Thou shall design logos in black and white before applying color

Commentary We have already established the fact that clients may react emotionally to the colors that we present to them. We have also laid out the need to create logos in such a way that they can be applied to a variety of items, from letterhead to signage to embroidery and everything inbetween. Now that we have talked through all of the pitfalls, it is the perfect time to give you a little secret into how to circumvent them. Working with your logo designs in black and white will help guarantee that the vector applications work well. Using only black and white while talking about the process with your client will also create solid acceptance of your design, without eliminating something because it was presented in an offensive color. Only the best designs will survive. Those conversations will also provide the base for your final color decisions. Often, both sides will find that they already know the colors they should use in the final solution. And never forget, if it works in black and white, it will work in most any color. **JF**

Thou shall remember that color + time can = brand

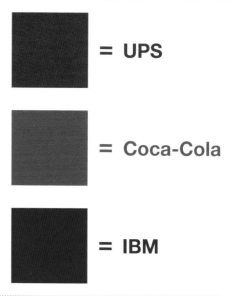

= UPS

= Coca-Cola

= IBM

Commentary One of the most incredible marketing efforts, tied directly to color, took place over the last few years. The shipping giant UPS has had the color brown as part of its identity since its earliest days, chosen for its dignified and professional appearance. Now, 80 years later, its entire campaign is based around simply calling the company itself "brown." This is a stunning acknowledgment of how important the color is to the way consumers identify and interact with the company. Built through constant reinforcement, from its delivery vehicles to its employee uniforms, UPS has owned brown in the marketplace to such an extent, and period of time, that they simply refer to themselves as such. This campaign stands as a vital reminder of how important color can be as a brand asset. It brings to mind companies with incredibly strong brands that lack in the logo department, and the decades built on instantly recognizing that Coca-Cola red on the supermarket shelf, among others. **JF**

Thou shall accept that there is no such thing as a bad color combination

Commentary Rules are meant to be broken. There are valuable and appropriate rules for color. But, once a designer reaches a level of proficiency and confidence with color, all rules are thrown out of the window. Bad color combinations are timid color combinations. The viewer will sense when a designer is unsure and inhibited. A small patch of violet on the page against an equally wispy patch of lime green will look like an error. Slamming violet and lime green together in a large and bold way will make them look exactly right. Van Gogh combined yellow with rust. In the hands of a lesser artist, timidly applying a small amount here and there, the solution would be bad. Van Gogh's *Twelve Sunflowers* appear perfect. As in most of life, doing something with bravery and self-confidence will always make others believe you are correct. **SA**

Imagery and Graphics

Thou shall not use stock images just to save money

Commentary Don't get me wrong here—I love the fact that we can go online nowadays and find 87,000 different shots of two businessmen shaking hands while grinning inanely at each other. This is ultimately a good thing because, if that's the kind of image you need for a project, the bulk availability and lower overheads of online picture libraries mean stock images are now a relatively inexpensive option. However, you should always think carefully about whether or not a completely unique image would serve your client better. Remember that other designers can download the same photos or illustrations you've selected for their own clients, and the better (and therefore more popular) images get pushed to the top of the list when you search by subject. If you think your client can afford original photography or illustration, always try to persuade them to consider that option first. It helps to keep the freelance community in work, too. **TS**

Thou shall always check to see if a perfect stock photo might be available

Commentary A very famous designer once told me a story about how one of his most iconic posters almost didn't come to fruition. It involved the interaction of a figure with a cityscape, only it had to be a specific city, immediately recognizable. He was limited in his options with the figure, so he joked to the client that should they want to rent a helicopter, he could easily get the image they desired.

They begged him to at least give it a try. He scoffed and thought about just telling them that he researched to no avail, so hopeless seemed the task. Then, he pecked out a quick stock search, only to discover a photographer who specialize in that region, leaving him with a multitude of options and an incredibly happy client, amazed that he could be so diligent in turning up such a difficult image to find. **JF**

Thou shall do your best to use client-supplied images

Commentary I see you staring at me, that slightly out-of-focus shot of the executive director and four other people that seem mildly important. One of them displays his expensive watch, and they're all drinking glasses of wine. I can feel you edging your way toward my precious magazine spread. The one I have been filling up with pull quotes and telling the client that there was no room for you inside. Besides the multitude of image edits you require, I take offense that you have been forced upon me. You can feel my disdain, but you move forward undeterred. When my back is turned, you inch directly on top of my monitor and whisper to me "I pay your salary." A bead of sweat arches across my forehead, as I realize I have been approaching this all wrong. As I turn closer, resigned to making you the best image you can possibly be, open eyes and exorcised drunks to the rescue, you smile and add, "plus, I come pre-approved." **JF**

217

Thou shall also show a client better alternatives to their own imagery if necessary

Commentary Most clients have not been educated as designers. They haven't studied the history of photography. They don't understand complex rules of composition. And they don't need to. Clients understand the rules of law, or medicine, or engineering. This may lead to a client supplying really awful imagery. It may be blurry photographs taken by a girlfriend who is interested in photography. It may be awful drawings of a client's pets, drawn by a relative. Or it may be as simple as a photograph that sends the wrong message. When the project is finished, there will be no note on the bad images that reads, "This was chosen by the client." The failure of the project will be the designer's. When faced with bad photography, art, or information graphics, the designer should find a better solution and present it as an alternative. Forcing this down the client's throat rarely works. Tactful and logical explanation, showing both alternatives is the correct approach. **SA**

Thou shall not assume that an image is good simply because it's been published on Flickr

Commentary Flickr® is a website devoted to the sharing of photographs. It allows people around the globe to upload their own images and share them with everyone else. Flickr and other websites that serve this purpose are remarkable tools to see into the lives of everyday people everywhere. Just because an image has been published online, does not make it good. There is no photography curator at Flickr accepting the wonderful images, and rejecting the bad ones. Flickr is not a source for stock images. Some images are remarkable, others images are horrible. The question one must ask is, "Would I hire my ailing mother to photograph this landscape image? Or would my four-year-old son be a good source for images of a holiday dinner? The answer will be no. Stock image websites are a good source for stock images. Using a photographer to shoot an original image is the best solution. **SA**

219

Thou shall not repulse your audience with imagery unless briefed to do so

Commentary Shocking images are a valuable tool for the graphic designer. An image that challenges the audience, or forces them to acknowledge an issue, is one of the strongest forms of communication. Repulsive and aggressive images are part of this canon. In the right context, this type of imagery can create a result that is spectacular. Repulsive images used for shock value alone are pandering.

The solution may receive the attention desired, but the lasting effect will be one of anger and negativity. If the client is the Sex Pistols, this response may be desired. Most clients, however, prefer a positive reaction. No communication is ever neutral. The response will always be clear or confused, positive or negative. The designer's role is to help guide that perception toward positive and clear. **SA**

Thou shall carefully consider the political content of all image choices

Commentary In the 1930s, the Nazi party began to censor art considered politically degenerate. Obviously, anti-Nazi art was the first censored. As time passed, the political content of 95 percent of art produced was deemed degenerate. In the end, the state only allowed benign landscape paintings to be exhibited. Every image has political content. A photograph of a group of people is immediately deconstructed by race, gender, age, and culture. Even a benign landscape painting can be seen as propaganda. Understanding the political implications of images, icons, and messages is a necessity for each designer. Is the curvaceous woman in a bikini holding a beer simply a picture of someone at the beach? Or is it, according to feminist theory, an example of objectification and oppression from a patriarchal culture? Each designer will need to determine this for him or herself. Purposefully using an image and recognizing its political subtext is a basic skill. **SA**

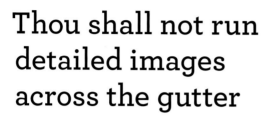

Thou shall not run detailed images across the gutter

Commentary A full-bleed image run across a spread in a book or magazine creates great visual impact and some pictures cry out to be used as large as possible. Magnificent landscapes or architectural shots can work really well, especially when they're overlaid with a strong typographic headline to open an article or chapter. Take care though, as it's easy to forget one vital detail—the gutter. When we design spreads we normally work "spread to view" so we can see left and right pages side-by-side. On a flat computer screen we tend to overlook the importance of the gutter because it's represented only by a fine rule, but in a bound magazine or book much of the viewable page immediately adjacent to the gutter can disappear into the spine. Images like those impressive landscapes can usually absorb this, but the cardinal sin is to chop through someone's face while positioning a portrait across a gutter. Don't cut off someone's nose to spite their face. Take care to ensure that gutters only pass through neutral image space. **TS**

Thou shall check that all images have an effective 300ppi resolution

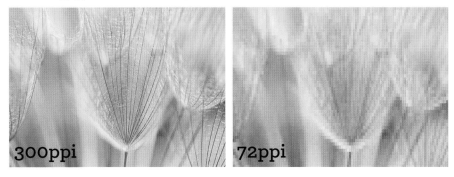

300ppi | 72ppi

Commentary The industry standard resolution for printing four-color halftones is 300ppi. I say ppi (pixels per inch) rather than dpi (dots per inch) nowadays as the vast majority of image reproduction involves a digital workflow and pixels are more representative of image resolution. It's generally accepted that the average human eye can't differentiate pixel densities beyond 300ppi, which explains why this is the recommended resolution for high-quality image reproduction. Other factors such as halftone screens (see Rule #228) also influence this choice.

So, you have your 300ppi image at, say, 4 x 6 inches. As long as you import the image to your layout at the same size (or smaller) you'll maintain a resolution of at least 300ppi and the print will theoretically look great. However, if you enlarge the image on the page you'll lose resolution. For example, enlarging the image to 8 x 12 inches halves the resolution to 150ppi, which will degrade the quality of the final print. The trick is, unless you have no alternative, never enlarge a 300ppi image beyond 100 percent within your layout. **TS**

223

Thou shall not import images with too high a resolution

Commentary We know that 300ppi is the industry standard resolution for quality printing, but what happens if we scan a halftone image at 600ppi? You might think it'll look twice as good when printed, but sadly you'd be wrong. It's true to say that in some cases slight improvements can be detected in images printed at a higher resolution than 300ppi but it's more of a fluke than anything else. The truth is, the extra resolution gets wasted and only serves to make the document size larger than it needs to be. In addition to this, banding (an uneven gradation of tone) can occur with images above 300ppi because the resolution doesn't correspond favorably with the commonly used 150 lines-per-inch halftone screen (see Rule #228). If you send PDFs to print rather than original layout files, there's a good chance that any imported images over 300ppi are resampled down to 300ppi anyway, but the issue of document size remains, slowing down all prepress processing and taking up extra space on your workstation or server. **TS**

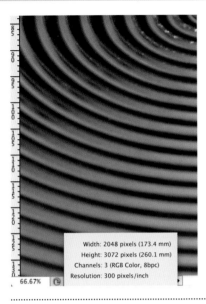

Width: 2048 pixels (173.4 mm)
Height: 3072 pixels (260.1 mm)
Channels: 3 (RGB Color, 8bpc)
Resolution: 300 pixels/inch

66.67%

Thou shall resample all images to 300ppi before importing them to a print document

Commentary When working on any book design project, I receive hundreds of images to choose from. Invariably, these images will be a mix of resolutions—some high resolution (300ppi) and others that have been shot digitally, which, although large dimensionally, are only 72ppi in resolution. If I were to place these latter images at 100 percent in my layout, I would in effect be placing low-resolution images into the artwork, which are never good enough quality to print with. It is essential, therefore, that you consolidate resolutions to ensure that all images you use are "hi-res." To locate the "lo-res" images before you import them to a layout, use software such as Adobe Bridge and adjust the resolution using Photoshop. If there are a lot, run an automated action in Photoshop to do the same, but make sure that you constrain the proportions with the resolution so that as you make them 300ppi, the images scale down correctly. Following this process means you can guarantee that every image will reproduce at at least 300ppi as long as you do not scale them above 100 percent in the layout. **PD**

225

Thou shall learn about digital file formats

Commentary We're really talking about the various *image* file formats here, all of which differ slightly and provide their own unique advantages. TIFFs (tagged image file format) remain a top choice for print workflows as they can accommodate embedded information such as alpha channels, meaning masks can be imported directly into a layout. Native Photoshop files are also a popular choice for the same reasons. JPEGs (Joint Photographic Experts Group) are great if you need to keep file sizes down but be careful how much compression you apply when saving as quality can suffer. A JPEG is also a bad choice if you think you'll need to edit the image further down the line as quality is lost every time you save a JPEG. Forget about EPS files (encapsulated PostScript) as they're rarely used now—go with native Illustrator files for vectors. PNGs (Portable Network Graphic) are popular formats for online use, offering the advantage of transparency support. I recommend some further reading as you may find you've not been using the best formats in your own image workflow. **TS**

Thou shall learn about bit depth

Commentary Bit depth is the number of bits, or binary digits, assigned to each pixel in an image. Bit depth isn't about resolution, it's about color quality—the higher the bit depth, the more tones you can achieve—so subtle color gradations improve as bit depth increases. Pure black-and-white images where each pixel is either on (black) or off (white) are termed 1-bit. Black-and-white halftones with gradations from black to white are 8-bit, so 8 bits of color information per pixel. Color RGB images are 24-bit because there are 8 bits of color information per channel, so 8 x 3 = 24. Photoshop can handle up to 32 bits-per-channel, or 96-bit images, but you'll find that many adjustments and filters won't work at this bit depth, and any extra quality provided may be lost during print. When working with 48- or 96-bit originals, it might pay to create a 24-bit copy for use in your layout. Check with your print supplier to see what they can achieve with their equipment. **TS**

Thou shall understand the relationship between resolution and image size

100%

600%

Commentary This is a pretty straight-forward relationship, unlike many of the domestic variety, but it's important to understand how resolution and image size affect one another. Any original image as recorded by a camera or scanner has its resolution set by the device. However, if you then resize it in InDesign so it's either more or less than 100 percent its original size, the resolution will change. A 300ppi image won't create more pixels when you enlarge it; the pixels will simply get bigger and more visible, thus reducing the quality of the reproduction.

For example, enlarging a 300ppi image to 600 percent within your layout will reduce the resolution to 50ppi. If you're interested in how the math works, it's 100 ÷ 600 x 300. Alternatively, just set your Links panel to list the *effective* ppi for imported images and you'll easily spot any with a resolution that has strayed beyond acceptable boundaries. You can get away with less than 300ppi if you have to, but don't make a habit of it. **TS**

Thou shall understand the relationship between image resolution and halftone screens

Commentary All four-color process images are made from dots and are alternatively referred to as *halftones*. A photographic print isn't made from dots and is known as a continuous-tone (contone) print. *Screening* is the term used to describe how a contone is converted to a halftone. The chosen print method and paper stock must be taken into account when selecting which halftone screen to use, with a higher value providing better print quality. A screen resolution of 150lpi (lines per inch) is standard for quality printing, while a newspaper will use a screen as low as 70lpi. The coarser screen will actually help prevent individual dots merging together when the ink spreads through the more absorbent newsprint. The relationship between image resolution and screen resolution is simple enough in that image resolution should be about twice that of the screen used, hence the industry standard of 300ppi and 150lpi. There's some leeway in the equation. Softer images without many straight lines or angles will stand up to coarser screening than anything containing much in the way of fine detail. **TS**

229

Thou shall choose images based on their appropriateness as well as their quality

Commentary Is it better to use a great shot that's not a perfect exposure, or a perfect exposure that's not quite the best shot? Ultimately the decision might not be yours as your client may value slick presentation over content quality, but for me choosing the shot that's the most appropriate is always the better decision. Think about all the wonderful images that have come out of field journalism where getting a perfect exposure hasn't always been the biggest priority. How about those accidental shots when you were doing the right thing by looking down the lens rather than at the settings on the back of the camera. When you look at the very best images, a pattern begins to emerge—content is king. Beautifully exposed images that are exactly right for a cover or spread are of course the perfect option, but it's wrong to choose an image purely because its technical quality is high. The reaction to a shot and the emotion it creates in the viewer must always take precedent. **TS**

Thou shall devise a system for the consistent naming of digital image files

0249_ComS.tif

Commentary It can be difficult when you are working on a large-scale project to manage and identify the many files that have been supplied. In some instances, a client or a publisher will have been very helpful and will have supplied the image files with logical and consistent names and in an organized manner. Often though, you won't be so fortunate, in which case it's worthwhile organizing the files and renaming them yourself before you import them. This will enable you to find and compare images and to maintain the correct links if the files are ever moved between workstations or servers. For book and brochure projects you may choose to use the chapter and folio numbers as a prefix for the image, so when listed alphabetically they appear in running order. However, if the pagination changes at some point this method may cause confusion, so a simple system of unique numbering and/or coding which doesn't follow a page order may prove to be more dependable in the long run. By taking stock of what you have and how the design is structured, a system of organization will become evident. **PD**

Thou shall work with Camera RAW image files

Commentary Adobe Camera Raw is, in a word, brilliant. If you shoot (or receive a shot) as a JPEG or TIFF it is what it is. You can adjust it, color correct it, resize it within reason, but that's basically it. Camera Raw is like having an old-style film negative because you can go back to the original to create new versions from scratch. A Camera Raw file contains all the raw data recorded by the camera at the point the picture was shot. Camera Raw files aren't compressed, nor are they subjected to any in-camera processing, so you can do a whole lot more with them right at the point when you first open them up in Photoshop's Camera Raw plug-in. You can reset temperature (or white balance), tint, exposure, brightness and contrast, clarity, and vibrancy, and a whole host of other adjustments. You can even open images at an increased size to the original, which can be very handy indeed. Ask your photographer for, or shoot in, Camera Raw whenever possible. **TS**

Thou shall utilize Adobe's DNG format when archiving images

Commentary We just mentioned how good Adobe Camera Raw is but it does have its limitations. The format is governed by the make and model of supported cameras, and the Camera Raw plug-in can't guarantee it'll support every camera forever. This means there may come a time when you won't be able to open an archived image. Enter the solution—Adobe's DNG (digital negative) format. Saving your images as DNG files removes the compatibility issue so they become "time proof," making them a much

better option for archiving, and you can still open them with the Camera Raw plug-in. The file sizes are slightly smaller too, which isn't a bad thing, and there are cataloging advantages to boot. If you drop a Camera Raw file into an image catalog, you don't see any of the adjustments you may have applied to the image, but with a DNG file the preview honors any exposure and color adjustments. This is a huge advantage if you choose to follow the advice in Rule #233 and create a DAM system. DNG is the way to go. **TS**

Thou shall use DAM to catalog image files

Commentary What's more boring, cataloging all your photographic images and illustrations or spending all day searching for that great shot that you may or may not still have on file somewhere? Personally I would say the latter is more boring and definitely more frustrating. Digital Asset Management (DAM) sounds like the dull option but it's actually really easy to do once you've got your system in place. You can buy specialist software like Extensis Portfolio, which creates standalone catalogs of all your images, or digital assets, as they all have potential commercial value. If you don't want to fork out for extra software you can use something like iPhoto, which comes as standard with every Mac, or Picasa, which is a free service from Google. Alternatively, you can just file images carefully in named folders and use Adobe Bridge for your image searches. Whatever system you go for, get to grips with *metadata*, which is defined as *data about data*. Use metadata to embed key words into your image files and tracking them down in the future will be a breeze. **TS**

Thou shall always apply some sharpening to digital images

Commentary On close inspection many images shot with a digital camera will appear to be slightly blurred. This happens because, just like the grain produced in shots from old-style film cameras, digital sensors produce a random speckling of tiny electronic dots across the shot known as noise. Digital cameras attempt to suppress noise by setting sharpness to the lowest acceptable level, which means that post-production sharpening is needed. Your photographer may do this for you as part of his or her contract along with any required color adjustments, but if not, the odds are that you'll be using Photoshop to do this yourself, so use Unsharp Mask or Smart Sharpen. Don't use the basic Sharpen filter as it's an all or nothing option and offers no real control over the end result. A word of warning— don't overdo it. Oversharpened images look worse than the "straight from camera" shot, so easy does it. Oh, one more thing, complete any and all image adjustments before you apply any sharpening. It should always be the last thing you do before importing the image to your layout. **TS**

235

Thou shall not crop well-composed images excessively

Commentary When an artist sits down at their easel to sketch out the composition of a painting, they're thinking carefully about what's happening at the edges of the work as well as what's happening at the center. Imagine how horrified they would be if they were to walk into a gallery, only to find that a picture framer had decided to chop 6 inches off the top of their work so it lined up nicely with the other paintings on the adjacent wall. Photographers do the same thing when they look through a camera viewfinder and compose the shot before they fire

the shutter, and photographic images should be treated the same way as paintings. Sure, not all photographs need to be treated with the same reverence, and some are shot with the intention they be cropped at will, but something like a fine landscape image or an immaculately composed portrait should be treated with respect and cropped as the photographer intended. It's kind of rude to crop heavily without good cause. **TS**

Thou shall not crop landscape to portrait and vice versa

Commentary Another professional's work should always be treated with respect. This is no less true when working with a photographer; their experience and creative "eye" for a good shot contribute to the careful composition and formatting of each photograph they produce. By taking their picture and recropping to a different format, more often than not you are degrading the overall quality of the image and negatively affecting its composition, as well as being disrespectful of their ability! Most photographers I know often take a landscape and a portrait of the same subject matter, with the orientation dictating their choice of composition. So check if there is an alternative before you start laying out your design. This rule goes for any type of image, art reproduction, or illustrated work, too. Meet the challenge and work with what you are given. **PD**

237

Thou shall use the right Photoshop tools for color adjustment

Commentary If you feel an image needs some color adjustment, it may well need a bit of tonal adjustment first. Color is directly affected by tonal adjustments because saturation will increase or decrease when darkening or lightening an image, so check *Levels* first. Don't bother with *Brightness and Contrast* as the adjustment isn't sophisticated enough. Drag the black and white point sliders of the Layers dialog in to meet the ends of the histogram to achieve good tonal balance. A *Color Balance* adjustment can solve simple color problems but for better results you need to study the workings of the *Curves* adjustment. It's not that complicated to get your head around and is arguably the most powerful adjustment tool in the whole kit. Read up about the popular S-Curve approach to color adjustment and you'll be well on the way to becoming a real pro. Knowledge of the color wheel will help you here, too. Here's a little side tip for any adjustment procedure. Decide what the worst issue is and deal with that first. It may be all that's needed. **TS**

Thou shall always edit images nondestructively

Commentary Since they were first introduced way back in 1994, Layers have always been one of the best things about Adobe Photoshop. In 1996 the functionality of the Layers panel took another leap forward with the addition of Adjustment Layers. Now, can you think of any reason why you wouldn't want to take advantage of what's termed *nondestructive* editing by using those wonderful Adjustment Layers? It's nondestructive because if you change your mind about any of the edits you apply you can readjust them or take them out completely, so this is a bit of a no-brainer, to be honest. However, some folks still manage to forget all about them and either apply adjustments directly to an original image or make endless saved-as versions of files in case they want to go back to an earlier version. This is, of course, completely crazy and pretty much inexcusable! As you can see I feel quite strongly about this one, so check out those Adjustment Layers and use them well, even for basic Levels or Curves adjustments. **TS**

239

Thou shall worship Smart Filters

Commentary We know that non-destructive adjustments are the way to go, as Rule #238 demonstrates. But what happens when we want to apply other effects without permanently changing the original image. When Photoshop® CS3 was released in 2007 it was the end of a long wait (after the arrival of Adjustment Layers) for the brilliant Smart Filters. Smart Filters are possible because of Smart Objects, introduced in CS2 to allow more flexible ways of working with scalable vector graphics, and are basically Adjustment Layers for filters. All you have to do is open your original as a Smart Object and apply whichever filters you care to choose. Each applied Smart Filter links in a stack to the selected layer and can be edited with Blending Options or reordered as many times as you like, or deleted completely if you decide you don't need it after all. They're applied as a Layer Mask, so you can also paint areas out to reveal the original image, without the applied filters. What's not to like about that? Smart Filters deserve the attention. **TS**

Thou shall eschew deletion in favor of masking

Commentary Returning to the theme of nondestructive editing, creating cutouts can also be given the same treatment through the use of Layer Masks. I prefer to keep as many previous workings of an image as is practical because you may for whatever reason need to return to an earlier version. On the flip side, I don't really like keeping dozens of files labeled version 1, version 2, and so on, so a mask carries the advantage of not deleting any data from an image. You can always revert to the original if needs be. In addition, tiny adjust-ments can easily be made to a Layer Mask with a small brush, and Photoshop's excellent *Refine Edge* function provides options for detecting, adjusting, smoothing, and feathering any selection. The one thing you always have to remember if you create a cutout with a mask is to check the *Save Transparency* box when you save the image. You also have to save as either a TIFF or PSD as JPEGs can't contain multiple layers. **TS**

241

Thou shall create clipping paths in Photoshop— not in InDesign

Commentary It's easy to create a quick clipping path in InDesign® using the built-in functionality, and it's equally as easy to create a frame directly from the resulting clipping path. This is fine for a quick one-off job that needs to be turned around in double quick time, or for something you're unlikely to come back to or edit. However, it's not really the best way to create a proper clipping path as it only affects the picture box used in your layout. Additionally, it's unlikely that the InDesign® clipping path will be quite so accurate as one you've first created in Photoshop® as part of the original image. Photoshop® provides so many more options for creating all kinds of paths, and allows you to refine and feather edges in ways that InDesign® doesn't. Remember, too, that if you use the image again elsewhere your cutout work is already done. Never try to create a clipping path from a polygonal picture box drawn directly in InDesign®. It's a really shoddy way of working and your print supplier will hate you forever so best not to, I reckon. **TS**

Thou shall always include a photography or illustration credit where it's due

Image © Tony Seddon 2011

Commentary A good editorial layout depends very highly on skillful use of space, good typography, and an eye for structure and navigation. However, if the piece is also illustrated, the images are more than likely the element that first elicits a response from a reader. The best layout in the world will never fully succeed if the images are only okay, and will fail miserably if the images are just plain bad. Given this, it's really only proper (and polite) to make sure the person creating great photographs or illustrations for a piece gets a credit somewhere. It doesn't have to be in 16pt text underneath every image, but if someone wants to check who shot the images for the fashion article or who created the cool vintage-look illustrations for the music feature, they should be able to do so. The majority of photographers and illustrators are freelance and need to publicize themselves constantly through the work they do for others, so it's important to try to provide that platform for anyone you work with. **TS**

243

Thou shall allow a photographer or illustrator to input creatively whenever possible

Image courtesy of Nikon

Commentary I've been fortunate to work with some incredibly gifted professionals in my career. These individuals are specialists in their fields and are extremely creative, knowledgeable, and experienced. So I've found it's always worthwhile listening to what they have to say, whether it be a suggestion or an observation. Invariably, their comments will add value and improve your project. Of course, you don't have to take on every suggestion they make, but it pays to listen as you never know what may come out of the discussion.

There have been a number of occasions when I've been on a photoshoot and the photographer and myself have struggled to get an image of a product to work. Despite our efforts, the shot just wouldn't come together, even though the initial idea was great! It's at times like these that open communication and a willingness to listen will benefit all parties and result in solutions that lead to successful work. **PD**

Thou shall not edit an illustrator's original work without permission

Commentary As with a photographer's work, it is important to be respectful of an illustrator's output. I've worked with many; if you brief them correctly and thoroughly, the work they produce will tick all the required boxes and often exceed your expectations. However, there will be the odd occasion where changes need to be made to the illustration, whether it's adding or removing elements, altering colors, or adjusting the size. In these situations, you should go back to the illustrator and ask for the changes to be done.

Not only is it more professional to do so, but the commissioning contract will often include a clause stating that you are not allowed to modify their work without permission. The last thing you want to do is start breaking the terms of a contract for what would appear to be a simple change. Go back to them, explain the situation, and they will nearly always accommodate any alterations. **PD**

245

Thou shall not do it yourself if you have a budget to commission

Image courtesy of Nikon

Commentary If there's a good argument to support why you should personally create illustrations or shoot photographs for a layout you're working on then fair enough. Perhaps you're genuinely the best choice for that particular task—no reason why you shouldn't be—but there's more to it than illustration and photography skills. Time is also a major factor and the more you decide to do yourself, the more time you'll need. I have a confession to make—in the past I've made bad decisions about how much

I should personally take on for a project when I could easily have delegated work to others while staying within budget. These decisions are sometimes driven by a desire to increase your personal stamp on a project, or simply that you really enjoy creating the images. Take a step back and answer the following question: Am I truly the best choice for the work and do I want to be in the office until 2a.m. tomorrow morning? If the answers are "maybe" to the first part and "no" to the second, pick up that phone. **TS**

Thou shall learn to use an SLR camera in case you have no budget for photography

Commentary Part of my education required that I take a color and black and white photography class. In retrospect, it was probably one of the three most important classes I have ever attended. Not only did it teach me some visual framing techniques, but more importantly, it made me comfortable holding a decent camera in my hands and expecting decent results to come from it. Little did I know that I would find myself jumping in to budget-ravaged assignments, shooting band portraits for CD packaging, menu photos for small restaurants, and anything desired, but financially unobtainable. I always use top people when needed, but that isn't always possible. Now, with everything digital, I shoot my portfolio as well, and not a day goes by when I don't shoot something for reference, or to use as a base to manipulate for an image or a texture in an illustration. I love my camera and it loves me back. **JF**

Thou shall not use your cell phone to shoot images for a project

Commentary I've often had to shake my head at the poor quality of images that have been supplied by some clients and have had to graciously return the images and ask them to resupply them. A common misconception is that pictures taken on low-grade cell phones will be of a good enough quality for high-end print purposes. Possessing limited resolution and lenses, these photos should be seen more as a "capture" than a photograph. Their lower quality will be evident when printed using offset litho or some other professional printing process and that's only acceptable if the project brief actually calls for this treatment. However, as with all things digital, technology moves on and many of the newer smart phones now available are capable of producing good-quality, high-resolution images which, up to a point, will be good enough to use. So, if you do need to use a cell phone for photography, ensure that the resolution of the built-in camera is high enough to capture detail and try to avoid camera shake when shooting. **PD**

Thou shall not use Photoshop filters to disguise a low-quality image

Commentary In school, a common excuse for missing homework is "the dog ate it." In graphic design, a common excuse for using the Solaria filter is, "the project needed it." Both excuses are obvious and pathetic. Nobody is fooled by the dog story. Nobody believes the image was wonderful, but the designer decided to Solarize it. Bad images are bad images. Low-resolution images are low-resolution images. There is no hiding from bad quality. This is an instance when requesting a better image is needed. Alternatively, a new image can be photographed. A solution can be executed with pencil, or cut-paper. And if all else fails, and a poor-quality image is the only option, use it big. Print it out and photograph it as a physical snapshot. Make the poor quality highly apparent and use it as part of the solution. **SA**

Thou shall not try to repair a bad image by desaturating

Commentary Desaturating an image is criminal. Perhaps, it is not legally criminal, but it is wrong. One of the tenets of modernism is to let materials be what they are. This means wood should look like wood, metal should be metal, and stone should be actual stone. There is no faux-painted marble in a Mies van der Rohe house. Bad images are bad images. Attempting to disguise one by desaturating it has one effect. It makes a bad image look desaturated. Sepia-toned photographs from the late 19th century look good because they are actual sepia-toned photographs. Taking an image photographed in the 21st century and making it sepia results in an image that is clearly artificially created. If the imagery is artificial and attempting to deceive me, why should I believe any of the text? The entire solution is compromised and has lost integrity. **SA**

Thou shall not scan a commercially printed image that has been screened

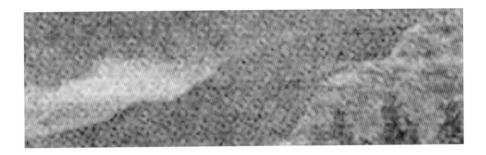

Commentary When a piece is commercially printed, the collection of CMYK dots that make up the base of the image form the visual you see. They can also form a moiré pattern when scanned afterward. Where a photo or a slide might be smooth and continuous, the printing process fragments this. It works to perfection on the intended final presentation, but when you try to drop that magazine cover in to your layout straight from the scanner, be prepared for a bizarre visual pattern to emerge instead of the hoped for image. The trick is to create a photograph of the image needed. Light that printed piece and be sure that it is squared up and as flat as is possible, with no flares or shadows. Take several photos, select the best, sharpen it digitally, and then you have a perfect file to work from. The extra steps are more than worth it. **JF**

251

Thou shall not enlarge images excessively "in layout"

Commentary When you're placing hi-res images in a layout, it's essential that you don't overscale them. Your hi-res files should have an image resolution of at least 300ppi, this being the correct resolution for screen rulings used in the litho printing process (see Rule #228). Increasing the scale of the placed image will reduce the image's effective resolution when printed. By way of an example, enlarging the image to 200 percent will reduce the resolution by half to 150ppi due to the doubling in size. If you need a larger hi-res to achieve the best layout—and you have knowledge that there may be better available—it's worth asking the client or the image source if one is available. If no replacement is forthcoming, then work with what you have. However, there is a small amount of leeway available. If the quality of the image is high you should be able to increase the scale when placed by up to 120 percent. You will find the majority of the detail, as long as it is not too fine, will be retained when printed, providing you with some flexibility in crop and scale. **PD**

Thou shall enlarge images incrementally in Photoshop

Commentary Take a look at the Image Size dialog in Photoshop and you'll see that there are different options to select when resampling an image. Photoshop has to create or delete pixels using clever things called *algorithms* when you resize an image. Extra pixels are based on the existing pixels, and a *Bicubic Smoother* is recommended for enlargements. This setting can give good results for enlargements of a fairly high percentage, but there is a limit. Some say as much as 200 percent is acceptable but I would say the

practical limit is actually lower. If you ever need to enlarge a digital image beyond, say, 50 percent it's a good idea to consider using the incremental enlargement technique. It's a simple process involving gradual increases in size of between 1 and 5 percent. Using small increments means Photoshop doesn't have to create as many new pixels for each enlargement, so color accuracy and clarity is maintained. For the best results always enlarge images in Photoshop first—never enlarge them in layout. **TS**

253

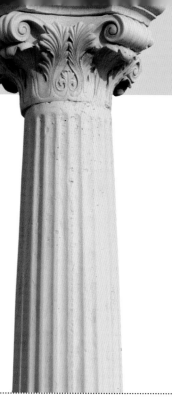

Thou shall choose images that support the text without repeating it

Commentary Many of us have attended a lecture where the speaker shows slides of his or her work. The worst speakers tell us what we see on the screen. A poster with a red headline and image of a hat appears on screen. The speaker says, "Then I made the headline red, and used a hat." If the audience is sight-impaired, this is acceptable. The best speakers show the work and expand on it with a story, situation, or hidden meaning. Text used as captions or headlines should give the viewer additional information. They should not repeat the obvious content of the image. As an example, a portrait of a man might have a headline such as "Wesley Thornton, Hero of the French and Indian Wars." A headline such as "Portrait of a man with a black shirt" only tells us what we already know. Images support the text, and the text supports the image. Each adds strength and information to other. **SA**

Thou shall keep icons simple and only expect them to convey a single idea

Commentary The Merriam-Webster dictionary defines an icon as follows: a sign (as a word or graphic symbol) whose form suggests its meaning. Successful icons communicate a singular and typically simple idea. A car on a winding road conveys the message, "Ahead, winding road." Poor icons attempt to communicate multiple ideas. In addition to the car and winding road, boulders may appear to be falling, and children may be seen running across the road. This is no longer an icon. This is now a painting. Many clients will want to say many things at once. The designer filters this information and returns with a clarified and more legible solution. **SA**

Thou shall know the difference between similar, example, symbolic, and arbitrary icons

Commentary We adore icons. As designers, we help place them all around us. It is important to know that icons fall into four specific categories, and to understand the separation. *Similar* icons are usually very literal and use simple objects, actions, or concepts. Many road signs fall into this category. *Example* icons usually convey a complex action in a single image. They usually use an image that we readily associate with a larger range of activity than the image itself, like a plane for an airport. *Symbolic* icons are used when an action or concept can be conveyed with a recognizable shape and are more conceptual, as the image often doesn't literally do what it is explaining, like a padlock for security. *Arbitrary* icons use imagery that must be learned to understand the meaning and bear little immediate connection to the concept that they convey. An obvious example is the icon for radioactive materials. **JF**

Paint Haus

Thou shall create logos that identify rather than describe

Commentary Each of us has a name. That name identifies us to the rest of society. Our first name may indicate our gender and origin. Our surname may indicate our cultural background. When introduced to Comte de Meux et Chalon Robert De Vermandois I might presume this person is a man from a French family. Queen Alfgifu of England would appear to be female and from a British family. Beyond these facts, however, I know nothing else. The names do not tell me if Comte De Vermandois is nice or mean, if Alfgifu is generous or thrifty. Good logos do the same job. Good logos identify an organization. They do not tell the viewer everything there is to know about the organization. The logo is the foundation of the visual system. It must exist in a variety of contexts. It should be able to withstand an advertisement to sell a product and a letterhead expressing condolences. Logos that describe are rarely legible, memorable, or accurate. **SA**

Thou shall create logos that work in print and online

Commentary Twenty years ago, designers made logos for print, and occasional environmental needs. The visual system required a two-color, one-color, and reversed version. Today, logos are applied to print, environment, broadcast, and online applications. The good news is that designers are now able to animate a logo, use a broader color palette, and think three-dimensionally. The bad news is that every logo needs to be legible on a printed piece and reduced to a small number of pixels online. A logo previously spent most of its life in a static two-dimensional world. Four-color logos were difficult and expensive to reproduce. A simple black and white logo with a two-color variation was preferred. Now, multicolored and three-dimensional logos are possible online. But, as in traditional print design, small hairline rules, delicate and tiny typography, and complex colors will not reproduce in print, and will fall apart on-screen. **SA**

Thou shall never use pixels when you can use vectors instead

Commentary Vector graphics have one massive advantage over pixel-based images—they're not resolution dependent, meaning you can enlarge them as much as you like with no loss in quality. Vectors are made using geometrical primitives, which are points, lines, curves, and polygons, and mathematical equations calculate how everything intersects. It sounds complicated but don't worry, the software does all the tricky stuff— all you have to do is draw the lines. They're not so good for the fine tonal gradations and subtle color shifts that bitmaps can handle, but for diagrams or logos they're perfect, and you can avoid the troublesome EPS (Encapsulated PostScript) file format nowadays as native Adobe Illustrator files can be imported directly into page layout programs. If it's possible to use vectors for an illustration or graphic (i.e., one that doesn't require the typical properties displayed by a photographic halftone), choose a vector approach every time and you'll never have to worry about any of the issues associated with resolution and image size. **TS**

Thou shall avoid Live Trace— it makes you lazy

Commentary Some designers are remarkable at drawing. These people were the students the art teacher asked, "Did you trace that?" This was not intended to be a compliment. This question pointed to laziness, deceit, and trickery. While Live Trace is an incredible tool technologically, it begs the question, "Did you trace that?" It is the tool of the weak and lazy. And it will always look like Live Trace. Especially disturbing are examples of handwritten letterforms that have been subjected to the rigid abuse of Live Trace. Recalling modernist tenets, allow something to be what it is. If handwritten text is necessary, write it, scan it, and use it. Using Live Trace will create forms that appear inauthentic. This deletes any spirit of spontaneity, or life. If an object needs to be drawn as a vector form, the designer should use the pen tool and draw the form. This controls any odd curves and stray points. It is the difference between a sloppy, careless approach and a meticulous and energetic solution. **SA**

Thou shall know that things that are noticeably different tend to be remembered

Dinner

Commentary When we stop and solve a problem, we are forced to engage with the issue. Elements that are unexpected or out of place create a problem that we must solve. Using an image of a baby with the word "Baby" below it, asks us to do little. Using an image of a baby with the word, "Dinner" below it, creates an emotional response, and we are left to question its meaning. This example will be remembered. While many people in the world may seem remarkably stupid while driving around us, typically they are able to solve problems. Speaking to the audience with a remedial tone is condescending and forgetful. Good design should not function like reading flash cards with simple icons and simple words to describe them. Good design asks questions, poses a point of view, and asks the viewer to complete the thought. **SA**

Thou shall understand the Face-ism Ratio

FABIA...
Artistic Director
Dance Institute of Washington
www.danceinstitute.org

Commentary Quite simply, the Face-ism Ratio is the ratio of face to body in an image, and how it influences the viewer in how they perceive the person in the image. The more face one can see in an image, the higher the Face-ism Ratio. There is specific math involved, if you are so inclined, but we are going to talk about the significance. This equation is hotly debated in terms of how it is used in regards to gender. In history, our images of men tend to be dominated by the face, emphasizing their personality and intellectual

qualities, and focusing squarely on character. Our images of women tend to show significantly more body, often the entire figure, focusing on their physical attributes and often with a sensual undertone. This is consistent across almost every culture. The point, as a designer, is paying attention to how much face you show in a cropped image, and being careful about what that conveys to the viewer. **JF**

Thou shall not allow any images above 105 percent to go to print

105%

Commentary In Rule #224 we discussed why you should ensure that images are 300ppi before you import them to a layout. In addition to this, you should ensure that the scale of the image does not increase beyond an acceptable amount once it has been placed. The rule that we are applying here is, never bigger than 105 percent. This is due to the fact that, as you increase the scale of the placed image, you are in effect decreasing its resolution, and therefore its quality. For example, if I place a 300ppi image at 150 percent, the image has increased by 50 percent in size over the original, or you could say the original takes up two-thirds the width of the scaled image. This now means that the resolution of the scaled image when output has decreased is no longer 300ppi but two-thirds the resolution, or 200ppi. This is a significant decrease and, when printed, the image quality will degrade. At a push, and if the image is very good quality, then 110 percent can be achieved, but stick with 105 percent and you'll be safe. **PD**

Thou shall not print images that are less than 300ppi

Commentary When sending a project to print, it's imperative to check that all images have a minimum 300ppi resolution. When publications and books are litho-printed, the printer will employ a screen ruling of 150–175lpi (lines per inch) to create the printing plates for the various colors. In order to calculate the required image resolution for the printer's screen ruling, simply double the lpi figure. Resolutions lower than 300ppi can sometimes be acceptable, depending on the project and paper stock, but it is generally accepted that 300ppi will work for most screen rulings, including finer screens of 200lpi, which would be considered for use on art books and monographs. The above, when coupled with the previous rule of not over-scaling images when placing into layout, will help to ensure that everything prints well. A quick and easy way to check your images is to use Adobe Bridge to collate and identify any files with stray resolutions. **PD**

Thou shall convert all images to CMYK before sending to the printer

 →

Commentary As has been discussed elsewhere in this book, the color printing process uses four colors: cyan, magenta, yellow, and black (CMYK), to reproduce color images and graphics. Many of the image files supplied to you, such as digital photographs, will have been created in RGB (red, green, and blue) mode, which is incompatible with the printing process (RGB-formatted images are used for screen-based graphics such as websites). Before you embark on converting them all, it is a good idea to talk to your printer. Not only is it possible to convert the images to CMYK—you can also add the correct CMYK profile to the images, which will be a great help to the printer, particularly if there are a lot of images. Simply find out which CMYK profile the printer intends to use and then carry out the conversion in Photoshop, thereby killing two birds with one stone. If there are a large number of images, you can run a batch of them through an automated action, saving you a lot of work and affording you the time to go and have a cup of tea. **PD**

Thou shall use a mixed RGB and CMYK image workflow

Commentary There's a vicious rumor kicking around that all images must be converted to CMYK before they're sent for reproduction and print. This isn't actually true—it's fine to implement a mixed RGB and CMYK workflow as long as you use color profiles. Color profiles (for example, *Adobe RGB 1998* or *FOGRA39*) contain data that describes how any one device, which could be a screen or a printer, will deal with the color information contained in an image. They use LAB, a device-independent color model (see Rule #163) to closely preserve colors that move from one color space to another. As most of us now send our artwork to printers as PDFs we can set Color Conversion to *Convert to Destination (Preserve Numbers)* when we export a PDF, helping to ensure that any RGB images in a layout convert automatically to CMYK while maintaining color consistency with the RGB original. This cuts out the need to convert all your images beforehand, and makes it possible to keep RGB originals which are better suited to color correcting and manipulation in Photoshop. **TS**

Production
and Print

Thou shall include 3mm of bleed on all artwork

Commentary If you elect to have full-page images that run to the edges of a page, they are referred to as *bleeding* off the page. When the page is trimmed, you must ensure that additional image content is provided past the page edge to avoid the potential for any white edges showing, due to the slight but inevitable variations that occur during trimming. This element of the artwork is called the *bleed* and should only appear on the trimmed edges of the book—it isn't necessary at the spine. I have been asked on occasion by a printer to provide 5mm bleed, but the norm is 3mm, allowing for those small degrees of movement with the cutters and the collated section as they are passed through the trimming machine. When you place your image and you're viewing it on screen, do remember that what you are seeing includes the bleed, so make sure that no important elements of the picture are too close to the trimmed edge or are going to be cut off altogether. **PD**

267

Thou shall always insist on obtaining a hard proof, even for mono print projects

Check

Proof has been checked and is:
- ☒ OKAY AS IS
- ☐ CORRECT AND SHOW NEW PROOF

Folding is correct as shown on proof:
☒ YES ☐ NO

REMARKS:

Commentary I know you think it is silly. A waste of time, or even worse, a waste of money—but when you stop and think about it, even the smallest job has enough time and money invested in it to make the cost of ensuring that it prints correctly negligible. How many times has someone been told that the PDF proof is written at a low resolution but it will be fine in the final printing, only to see one little photo or logo that ripped at a 72dpi preview included? Catalogs and shopping flyers are full of these mistakes. Even the very best printers sometimes have technology foil their efforts, or they rush a soft proof out, only to have everyone be sorry in the end. It is always the right choice to review even the simplest job properly. Always. **JF**

Thou shall attempt to run color proofs on the correct paper stock

Commentary Every designer has faced a situation when a client insists the color of the printed piece is wrong. The client is convinced they saw a proof that was perfect, and now the color is wrong. There are several reasons why this could occur: First, clients remember what they want to remember. Save the proof and show the comparison. Second, the printer made an error. Go on press on each job to verify the correct color. And third, the color proofs were on the wrong paper stock. The designer showed the client proofs on a white-coated stock, and the job printed on an uncoated cream stock. The solution is simple; always show the client proofs on the correct, or similar stock. Explain the differences between digital proof color and offset printing. They are entirely different technologies, and will never match exactly. If the printer provides an ink drawdown, make sure the ink is printed on the exact paper to be used when printing. **SA**

Thou shall not use laser printers to produce color proofs

Commentary As described earlier, in much the same way as you wouldn't specify a color for print based on its on-screen appearance, the use of color lasers should not be relied upon at all to provide an accurate color representation. I've found that color lasers are great for checking that all the elements are in place and I would always be happy if a printer supplied them to me for signing off on content and editorial changes, but they should never be used for color. The first reason for this is that the process is entirely different from litho printing and is much cruder. Litho is an ink-based process using a combination and arrangement of ink dots which when combined creates a high-definition output. Lasers are toner-based and overlay the colors in a more "instant" and opaque way, lacking refinement and accuracy with both color and images. The second problem with lasers is the machines themselves. They are in constant need of calibration, and I have found that factors such as temperature and toner levels greatly affect the color output. **PD**

Thou shall not accept a soft proof unless time saving is more important than quality

PROOF >>> PROOF >>> PROOF >>> PROOF

Commentary Life is about compromises. Business is about balancing those compromises. Design is about trying to keep those compromises from savaging the integrity of our projects. So, it is with great pain, after we have extolled the necessity of seeing a hard proof on even the simplest business card, that we offer one up to the compromise gods. We make most of our decisions in regards to how wonderful a final project will eventually be around time. Will we have time to do things the right way, to truly give them thought and exploration? Even when we find the answer to be yes, we have our legs cut out from under us by an accelerated production schedule. Few things in this day and age are not weighed down with the expectation that they were to be delivered yesterday. So, we look compromise hard in the eye, and we weigh time versus quality. We fight for quality, but we know that a project that delivers after an event has occurred is of little use to anyone. **JF**

271

Thou shall never assume the printer will understand exactly what you require

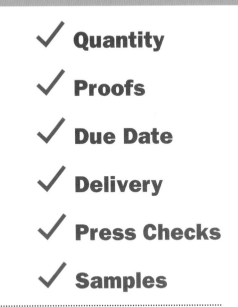

✓ **Quantity**

✓ **Proofs**

✓ **Due Date**

✓ **Delivery**

✓ **Press Checks**

✓ **Samples**

Commentary There are many extraordinary printers. These are the printers who are committed to meeting deadlines, providing honest and quick answers, and are immaculate in their craft. Then there are printers who might as well be Rhesus monkeys. Some people may walk through life trusting others, and believing that most others have the best intentions, and want to do good. This is a great, albeit frightening and naïve, attitude in day-to-day life. To believe this with all printers is foolish. Designers may be good at communicating the client's problem, but can be less than clear with printers. Assuming the printer will use a specific paper stock, add varnishes, bind the project, and deliver it to the client is risky. Pretend that a Rhesus monkey at the printer is handling the job. Itemize every aspect of the project: quantity, proofs, schedule, delivery, press checks, and processes. Do not assume anything, ever. In the end, the printer will appreciate the clear direction, and there will be fewer surprises. **SA**

Thou shall get your printer involved as early as possible in your project

Commentary You seem like a pretty smart cookie. Are you able to keep up on every innovation in design and advertising, from software to philosophical trends? Of course you can't. No one can fully keep abreast of their vocation, much less another field altogether, no matter how related it might seem on the surface. Printing and design, though they often hold hands, are wildly different industries. Recognizing that you should know enough to have an intelligent conversation with your printer, but could never imagine that you would fully understand the ins and outs of the business, is a good start. The sooner you engage your printer in your project, the quicker they can enhance it, adding special techniques, innovations in the industry, or better yet, cost savings while still delivering an amazing product. Or, letting you know of delays or complications in specifying certain materials. It makes all the difference. **JF**

273

Thou shall confirm that all materials from the client fit specifications immediately upon receipt

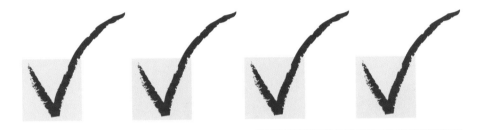

Commentary Is there anything more frustrating than cooking a huge meal and finding that your spouse picked up regular sugar rather than the required brown sugar on the shopping list? Building the extension on your home and putting the new window into the frame, only to find out that it is 90 percent of the size needed? There actually is something more frustrating—hiring a catering company to cook that meal, or a contractor to complete your build-out, only to be told that the job can't be done with the materials on hand. Even though you watched them take receipt of said materials days, weeks, even months beforehand. This is the way your client feels when you ask for a bit of copy, or an image in a higher resolution, right before the deadline for a project. Not only have you let them know that you didn't start on the job until the last minute, but you come across as unorganized and not detail-oriented, as is vital in this business. **JF**

Thou shall build contingency into all printing schedules

Commentary In Switzerland, trains run on schedule. In printing, things happen that delay a project. A client may have last minute alterations. The press may break. The ink color might be flawed. The paper shipment may be delayed, or incorrect. Printing is a physical process that involves people, trucks, machines, ink, and paper. It is not an instant solution like a digital printer on a desk. There are too many components and people involved for a job to never have even a small issue. The project might be delayed because the client decided to change a word in a paragraph just as the job began printing. This requires the job to be pulled off the press, new files created, proofed, and approved, additional paper ordered, new printing plates created, and the job rescheduled on press. This one small change could delay a job by 24 hours or more. Unfortunately, the client will not recall that he made the change. He will only remember that the designer didn't deliver on time. Add time into the printing schedule to create a buffer for the unexpected. **SA**

iCal

Calendars +

Day | Week | **Month** | Year

April 2012

| 26 | 27 | 28 | 29 |
| Additional stage for final layouts | | | |

2	3	4	5
Revised week for client approval			Good Friday
	Files due at printer		

Thou shall pass scheduling issues on to your printer as soon as they occur

Easter Monday

Commentary As much as we love our work creating cool and sexy designs, a big part of our role (and I emphasize BIG here) is managing the production process. One of *the* most important parts of this is liaison and communication with the printer. It's imperative that, if the "goal posts" move with scheduling, the information is passed on to the printer immediately as it can have a disastrous impact on any production schedule. Quite often a client will ask if a delivery schedule can be brought forward or moved back slightly; never say yes until you have checked with the printer. Confirming a schedule when it cannot be achieved will be disastrous as you would have made a commitment that cannot be kept, breaching the trust of the client and putting yourself in an extremely difficult position. Maintain open and honest communication at all times and, if things change, get on the phone immediately, ask the right questions, and give the client the correct answers. **PD**

Thou shall keep an off-site backup of all live projects

Commentary When disaster strikes, you don't know what will happen to your premises or assets, so make sure you have a backup of your work somewhere off-site. If your studio gets flooded, say au revoir to any computers that go for a swim, and if your studio backups get damaged then you are in worse trouble! The same goes for fire, and with theft they are just spirited away so you will have no opportunity of recovering any hard drives for data. Backup software such as Apple's

excellent Time Machine are a must. Providing yourself with an off-site backup gives you a guarantee to recover all of your lost data and get yourself up and running much quicker. Many years ago I learned the hard way when my studio was burgled and cleared out of Apple computers. Fortunately, we only lost three days' worth of studio time, having just carried out a large backup of the workstations but it was a lesson I never forgot! Data is your livelihood so protect it at all costs. **PD**

277

Thou shall archive meticulously at all times

Image courtesy of LaCie

Commentary If you spent six months building a perfect scale model of the *Titanic* you would make sure it was put in a solid case to protect it, while hoping it would last longer than the original ship. You should feel the same about the design work that you spend weeks or months creating for your clients. All the work you create is potentially an asset and, while you can't supply the exact same layout over and over to all your clients, a great deal of design work can become return business—for example, updated editions of brochures or newsletters. If you leave this material lying around on your computer desktop or on unmarked DVDs at the bottom of your desk drawer it's likely that you'll not be able to locate it when you next need it. It'll be a start-all-over-again moment—not good. Invest in a good-quality external hard drive for archived material and, better still, keep an off-site backup on DVDs as well. **TS**

1 × CD IN A CARD | 128.5

1 × CD 32pp BOOKLET
1 × CD IN A CARD WALLET   128.5

1 × CD IN A CARD WALLET   122.5

126   11   126   16   127

BACK   FRONT

129   13   129   35   332.5

GLUE FLAP

GLUE FLAP   25   GLUE FLAP   25   GLUE FLAP   25

Thou shall obtain a printer's template before beginning a packaging design assignment

Commentary Every manufacturer has its own nuances to consider. No matter how many music packaging projects you have completed, every vendor will have a slight variation in size and where the folds and scores occur. It is not noticeable in the marketplace, but it could be the difference in the placement of huge portions of the design. A left panel now becoming an upside down top panel, bleeds and glue panels in radically different positions. Every bag of coffee beans has a gas release in a different spot, meaning a bump and hole could suddenly emerge in the middle of your layout. Even little boxes of soap close in different configurations across the board. I could go on for days. The point being, save yourself the huge nightmare of reconfiguring your designs to wedge on to a template; get one from the printer to work over. Then, you can embrace it and design something special around its little quirks. **JF**

Thou shall assemble a full-scale mock-up of any packaging/ dimensional project

Commentary Building a house on your computer screen is a long way from planting a shovel and moving earth. On a smaller scale, the same is true about designing anything dimensional, especially packaging. What looks like it might work structurally doesn't bend as planned, lock together, or even stand up straight. Even after you have made adjustments and tested out the very core structure, you find the more nuanced aspect of designing in this way. How does a small piece of type read now that you know it will sit back a little on the shelf? Should the name of the product bend around to the point that you can't see all of the letters unless standing in a specific spot? How does the design work at the folds and seams? Where does the legal copy sit? After all that, does it fit in the needed shipping containers and the commercial display cases and shelves? Test, test, test. **JF**

Thou shall request a paper dummy from your printer

Commentary I love paper samples and it's always great thumbing through them and deciding which materials are appropriate and how they can be employed in a project. Once you get a final list, it is worthwhile getting a dummy made up, whether it be for a brochure or a book, so you can better judge how production factors may impact on your design. I also think it is important to show dummies to clients so that they know what to expect when the final item arrives. It may be that they have something else in mind or would prefer a different material for the cover or interior pages, and it is much better that they have a chance to comment at an early stage. Otherwise, you risk receiving comments once the final product has been delivered, such as "Oh . . . I think the text pages are too light." **PD**

281

Thou shall learn about dot-gain for different paper stocks

Commentary As far as a digital image file is concerned, dot-gain doesn't exist. Every dot making up a digital halftone image will stay exactly the same size no matter how many times you duplicate it. However, when you physically transfer the image to paper it's a different story—they get bigger and the image or color tint gets darker. There are various reasons why dot-gain will almost always occur regardless of the paper stock used, but the main culprit is ink absorption during the drying process. Printing on coated stock will diminish the effect caused by dot-gain as the paper is less absorbent and the ink spreads less. This doesn't mean that high-quality print should always be paired with coated stock as dot-gain can, of course, be compensated for using press profiles matched to your printer's machines. Screen ruling plays an important role in the process; coated stock can cope with values from 150lpi to as much as 300lpi, standard "matt art" paper 15–175lpi, lightly textured stock 120–135lpi, and so on. For newsprint, a screen ruling as low as 85lpi is about right. **TS**

Thou shall appoint printers that already know what "dot-gain" means

Commentary When you work with low-price printers, one of the common issues is that your job returns darker than expected, especially when you specify uncoated paper, as explained in the previous rule. This is a sure sign that your printer has either not accounted for, or doesn't understand, dot-gain. When this happens across all four plates in process printing, it can account for as much as a 20–30 percent shift in how dark the final color can be. As we learned in Rule #281, dot-gain can shift between paper stocks, and vendors take great care to provide information to help printers so that their sheets perform as best as they can, working with their prepress departments. This needs to be factored into how the individual presses run, and sometimes how the operators run them. It is absolutely essential in getting optimum results from your printer that they understand this, and understand how to control it. Never assume that a printer will take the necessary care this issue demands. **JF**

283

Thou shall investigate whether to overprint or knock out additional spot colors and metallics

Commentary Adding in a fifth color can be the defining point in a project. Whether it is a spot color to keep consistent color across several pieces, or to hold tight to corporate branding, or a shiny metallic or fluorescent providing maximum bang for the visual buck, once you have made that move, the most important decision is whether to overprint the additional color, or knock it out and trap it. Be sure to talk to your printer and get their advice, factoring in the sheet you are printing on, as well as the expected results. Individual colors can require different considerations. Metallic silver ink can have an issue with trapping against dark colors and images, overprinting can mean laying on the ink thicker to hold opacity, compromising small or fine type, whereas knocking out can allow for tight control in those areas. Big impact. Important decisions. **JF**

Thou shall run advance test proofs when utilizing unusual printing techniques

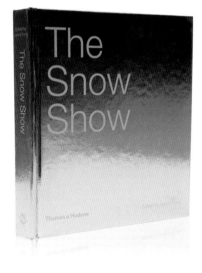

....

Commentary I always like to err on the side of caution if the design incorporates any unusual printing techniques or a method that requires quite a lot of advance preparation to ensure that it prints correctly. A process that I always test proof in advance would be a foil-blocking (or any other type of blocking for that matter) to ensure that the block has been correctly made and that there are no faults contained within the etching. In addition, you get to see the color of the foil so a change can be made if needed. The same goes for color palettes. Although not an unusual printing process, I try and get a test proof done of the colors and their tints, with a number of type treatments employing the colors so I can see how they work when applied to typographic elements. It's a far safer way to do it and, again, the client can comment well in advance of the actual project being sent to print. **PD**

285

Thou shall consult publications' specifications prior to designing an advertisement

Commentary Magazines, newspapers, and publications that use advertising have strict policies regarding the artwork for ads. They may seem arbitrary, sensible, or ludicrous. But this is their magazine, their art department, and their choice. Before designing an advertisement, consult with the publication and request an artwork specification sheet, and the exact ad order placed. Regardless of who purchased the ad space, the designer must verify the size and requirements. Unbelievably, people sometimes make mistakes. They think they purchased a full-page ad, but actually ordered a $1/2$ page version. The artwork specifications will clearly state trim size, bleed, ink requirements, screen size, and any other pertinent issues to the production of the magazine. Turning over an ad that is RGB, the wrong size, and the wrong resolution is dangerous and wrong. **SA**

Thou shall ensure that all text in black is set to overprint background colors

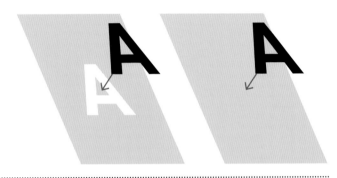

Commentary When I am designing books they are often to be co-editioned (translated into foreign-language editions) so the English text is run as a special black, which *overprints* the remaining elements on the page. That way this plate can simply be removed and a German or French edition can be overprinted in its place. However, even if your work isn't going to be translated it is still important that all black text sitting on a colored background should overprint. If you don't overprint the black text, it will "knock out" of the background (i.e., there will be a reversal in the color for the black text to sit into). This can cause registration issues, especially if the text elements are small in size, say for folios, captions, and even body text. To make the text overprint in InDesign, select from the palette menu: Windows > Attributes. Highlight the text and click the check "Overprint Fill." You can preview the effect under View in Overprint Preview. Of course, this treatment works with any color, so have fun experimenting. **PD**

287

Thou shall always include crop and registration marks with artwork for print

Commentary In order for a printer to trim the page correctly and match up the printing plates so they are true, the inclusion of these marks is essential. With most current DTP software, the inclusion and output of these marks is easy—literally a few clicks of a button at the print output stage and they will be incorporated. Usually, a printer will do this if you are supplying the source files and related hi-res images. However, an increasing number of

printers require PDF files. When creating PDFs, it's important that you remember to incorporate crop and registration marks. Items that are to be die cut, such as a folder, not only need crop marks and registration marks but also a "cutter guide" (an outline of the element to be cut out) for the printer to follow. **PD**

Thou shall own a copy of, or subscribe online to, *The Chicago Manual of Style*

Commentary What if there was a book on your shelf, or a website you could go to, that could answer nearly every single question you could ever have about American English. Something to cut short all those emails, texts, forum postings, asking friends, relatives, co-workers, strangers what a certain proofread mark means, or when to use a certain form of punctuation. A guide for editors and writers alike, and those of us who deal with copy every day. Surely, you would own such a book, or have access to such a site. If only someone would put such a thing together, and update it regularly to keep pace with the evolution of language and grammar. Wait a minute. You say such a thing already exists? That's right, the University of Chicago Press has been publishing the essential guide since 1906, and has gone through 16 editions and counting. You need this. Run, don't walk. **JF**

289

Thou shall set up folios on master pages

A Production and Print

Commentary Earlier we talked about the benefits of employing master pages in long documents, particularly with respect to how they can save time and guarantee consistency for common and repeated items on the page. Another key feature of master pages is the ability to set up automatic folios. The folios can be styled up how you wish them to be, with font, size, and color all adjustable. The insertion of a special character (in InDesign this is referred to as "Current Page Number" under "Markers") then allows for the pages' folios to be auto-numbered. These folios can still be adjusted when on the page—or deleted by unlinking them from the master—but adjustments made on the master pages will still affect them. If you need to move pages around, fear not—by moving spreads around and repositioning them the folios will renumber instantly, giving you one less thing to worry about or attend to! **PD**

Thou shall press check every project possible, even business cards

Commentary Once, while visiting a massive mansion, I was struck by the bathroom sink having had the knobs for the water installed backwards, so that it was unnatural to reach across to turn them on and off. I was certain that, despite the gorgeous and extravagant structure all around it, I could never live in this house with it tormenting me so. It reminded me that no part of a job is too small for proper supervision and attention to detail and a failure can ruin everything around it. Press inspecting a job allows for the designer to make adjustments, as well as ensure that all the elements are in place, every "t" crossed. In a worst-case scenario, you merely make certain that the job prints as expected. In a best-case scenario, you can improve the final product, popping a color, matching to another piece, and making it all that it can be. **JF**

Thou shall match paper stock to the appropriate printing technique

Commentary Ideally, you should be able to choose from as wide a range of paper stocks as you wish when planning the print side of a project, but sometimes the printing process will narrow down your choice. For example, sheet-fed offset lithography requires paper with good surface strength, which in turn provides good dimensional stability. Paper stock that stretches during full color printing is a recipe for disaster as mis-registration will occur between each color as it is laid down. Other factors to take into account are smoothness, absorbency, opacity, and compressibility. Standard stock sizes for sheet-fed processes are also important; will they fit your suppliers press and how much will be wasted during trimming? The paper is more often than not the most expensive component of any print project, so do your research early and always choose your paper stock with care. **TS**

292

Thou shall be aware of paper show-through

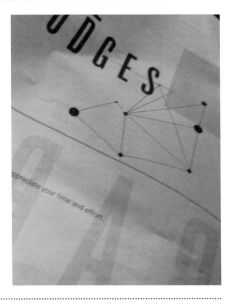

....

Commentary Few things send me off into a fit of giggles like a woman wearing white pants over dark underwear, unintentionally (let's hope) showing the entire world the outline of her unmentionables. When said undergarment has a pattern of hearts or polka dots on it, the giggles become uncontrollable. Juvenile behavior for sure, but who can blame me? The simplest miscalculation means that everyone around her will only notice one thing, and that one thing is the item that she had no intention of sharing, much less distracting all comers with.

This generally happens when someone gets dressed in poor lighting, when the sheerness of the outer garment is not noticeable, only to emerge into the sunshine, or bright commercial lighting, and give all eyes a bit of a surprise. Paper show-through works in much the same manner. Exposure to light affects the opacity, and thin sheets in particular can allow for the image/text on the page behind it to "show through" to the one you are viewing. **JF**

Thou shall ask your printer for the panel sizes of a folded leaflet

Commentary There are dozens of different ways to fold leaflets and brochures, the only restriction being the sheet sizes of paper stock and the available folding machinery your printer can access. Folding sequences become more complicated as the number of panels increases, which may seem obvious, but it's not just because of the panel count. Those panels that fold in on themselves need to be sized differently to allow a leaflet to lie flat when completely folded. Take for example the Wrapped Accordion fold, a standard accordion enclosed by

integrated front and back covers which will be the full width of the folded leaflet, let's say 4 inches or 100mm. Other panels folding into the cover need to be slightly narrower, allowing them to fold inward but still fit comfortably. The recommended reduction in width varies between sources but something in the region of $1/12$ inch or 2mm should do the trick. The weight of the paper stock also has a bearing on the amount of adjustment needed. The bottom line is, always request a template from your printer. **TS**

294

Thou shall work in halftones and vector when silk screening

....

Commentary For ages, silk screening was thought of as one of the roughest forms of printing. As new generations of designers have come to embrace those very qualities, along with the economics of making short-run projects, from posters and t-shirts, to most anything you can imagine pressing up against a screen to have ink pulled along it, it has emerged as a powerful niche. Currently, it is so popular that I am working on something being produced via screen print every day. I love the thick ink and the way no two pieces are quite the same. It is the polar opposite of process commercial printing. But, I have to be mindful that it also differs at the production end. The way screens are created/burned requires that all art be either vector- or dot-based, and exist at 100 percent of the color. That positive is what creates the portion in the screen that lets the ink through, and shades are not an option. It requires a complete rethink in how you approach your design and production. **JF**

Thou shall always have up-to-date paper swatch books

Commentary Paper companies have long used the swatch book to show off the capabilities of their sheets, combining current design trends with flashy techniques, in the hope that you will choose their line, and put it into use on a stunning final product. Most studios, firms, or in-house departments will eventually have a printer visit their office, who will notice that they don't have all of the current swatch books, and will see to it that some are delivered. Making sure that swatch references are up to date is vitally important. One day in the future, you may go to spec a sheet and find that a swatch doesn't exist any longer, or that that finish is gone, or the weight of paper is no longer available. Paper companies are all too happy to send these to you. Take advantage. **JF**

296

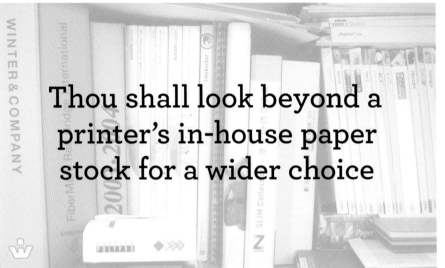

Thou shall look beyond a printer's in-house paper stock for a wider choice

Commentary There are many paper and materials manufacturers out there and it's beneficial for the graphic designer to be aware of the range of print companies and products available. There are times when a concept may be driven by, or nearly always enhanced by, the materials the designer chooses; often, with an unusual print process thrown into the mix, a really successful and powerful end result can emerge. Getting to grips with what's available is fun and all the paper makers have swatch books and printed examples available to be sent out. They usually offer a samples service whereby with a quick call you can order larger sheets to help you make decisions on specifications or use for mock-ups and presentations. Don't limit yourself to companies that exist in your home country. There are truly fabulous papers available from around the world and all can usually be shipped in bulk to your printer. **PD**

Thou shall familiarize yourself with international paper sizes

Broadsheet

Tabloid/Ledger
Letter

A6   A0

Commentary To enable designers, clients, and printers to discuss matters of specification and pricing on a level playing field, it is advantageous to establish an understanding of available paper sizes. Standard U.S. and European paper sizes do differ so it's worth getting an overview of how the respective systems work. The U.S. paper sizes are based on multiples of 8 ½ x 11 inches (or *Letter*), but some sheets will be a little larger to allow for images that bleed and to allow for grip when on press. In Europe the system most widely employed is ISO 216 and

is based around "A" formats. The A sizes are ordered downward in size, being approximately half the area of the next size in the range, with A0 at 1 m^2 and A6 at just 155.4 cm^2. In addition, the "C" series provides formats for envelopes and postcards, where a C4 envelope is slightly larger than an A4 sheet. Finally the "RA" and "SRA" ranges provide untrimmed format options for commercial printers which are slightly larger than the "A" sizes and, once again, allow for grip when on press. **PD**

Thou shall not specify cheap paper stock

Commentary It is said that salt is salt. But if you are a chef, you will explain that salt from the grocery store is different from refined salt from New Zealand. Paper is similar. Civilians will say, "Paper is paper. Isn't it all the same?" Designers, like a gourmet chef, know the difference. Paper stocks vary in tone and surface. They range from sheets made of 100 percent post-consumer waste to very little recycled material. Cheap paper will be, yes, less expensive, but the resulting product will never match a higher-quality paper. A cheap paper will not accept ink as well. There may be scoring and folding issues. And there will be deviations in brightness and whiteness from one sheet to another. Unless the job has an incredibly low budget, or the quantity is enormous and paper costs are a large fraction of the budget, never scrimp on paper. The end product may be slightly more expensive, but will be infinitely more successful and the client will be pleased. Alternatively, the client might save some money, hate the final product, and the designer will be fired. **SA**

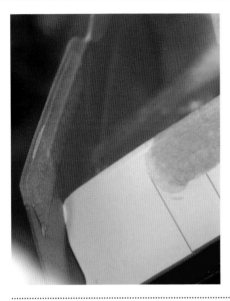

Thou shall know where the glue sections are and make sure that they are ink free

Commentary Do you know what glue likes to stick to? Paper. Do you know what glue doesn't like to stick to? Ink. It seems like it should be simple enough to keep the two apart. However, the glue area on most pieces and products falls on the inside of a fold, requiring that there be a bleed so that the design can be seen in full and the package can sport a finished look, rather than awkward paper stock peeking out at the seams. Mail pieces might need to ultimately close on an open page or envelope, with complicated folds, making it a simple step for the end user. That means that the areas where glue will go down in the production process, as well as those where the user may place it, need to be well thought out and marked early on. Once that happens, be sure to take extra care to keep them clear. **JF**

300

Thou shall understand when to use different binding techniques

Commentary There are a number of different commercial binding techniques that offer varying aesthetic qualities and practical applications. Which technique is best for your project depends upon specifications such as page extent and format. For example, an A4 40-page concert program can either be "stitched to wires" or "perfect bound" (glued pages into the cover). The use of case binding for a hardcover book, where the pages are collated in sections and held in place by use of an endpaper, would be wholly inappropriate. Firstly, you don't have enough pages for the cover to physically work (the thickness of the pages when collated is too thin to allow the binding to be "built".) Secondly, even if it were possible, the cost would be prohibitive; case binding is a much more expensive process to employ. So you not only need to consider the suitability of the binding to the project but also the cost implications. **PD**

Thou shall not saddle-stitch an extent more than 96 pages

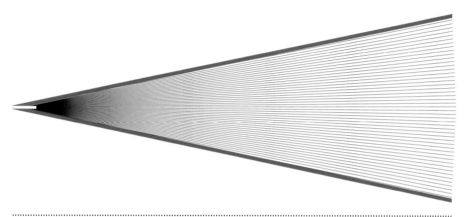

Commentary Saddle stitching is an alternative term for wire stitching or simply stapling. The staples used for saddle stitching are different to those you use in the office-style stapler you have sitting on your own desk. They're longer and are made from a rounder profile wire, usually in stainless steel to prevent rusting, which is fed from a roll rather than a clip. It's called saddle stitching because printed sections are placed over an inverted V, like a sharp saddle, prior to being stitched together on the bindery production line. It's the most popular way to bind magazines or brochures because it's the cheapest and is also much quicker than other binding procedures. However, there is one important restriction—it can only handle a limited number of pages. If a publication's extent goes beyond the 96 page mark, an alternative method will be required. Once again the weight of the paper stock must also be taken into account, not only because of page extent, but also to account for the unavoidable "creep" (see Rule #302) which will occur. **TS**

302

Thou shall ensure layout allows for "creep" at trim and spine when binding

Commentary *Creep*? And no, we're not talking Radiohead here. When a book or brochure's pages are folded together or collated into sections prior to being bound, and as the pages are stacked together and increase in number, the gauge of the paper forces the inner sheets out until they are sitting proud of the outer sheet. The result when trimmed: the inner's outer margins will be thinner than the outer's. Not only will this be unpleasant on the eye but also any items dangerously close to the trim edge could be cut off. Similarly, one must be wary of the binding mechanism specified, as some techniques use up more of the gutter of the page than others. An example is perfect binding, where up to 5mm of the gutter margin on the page can be lost. When deciding on your layout and working out the margins, consider the page extent and the binding so that you can counteract that dreaded "creep"! **PD**

Thou shall use matte and gloss lamination appropriately

Commentary Lamination is the most popular technique used for finishing the covers of books, brochures, and magazines. It provides additional stiffness to the chosen paper stock and it helps to protect the printed cover from dirt and marks. Lamination can be applied in the form of a film, which is glued to the stock by passing it through a heated roller, or by the application of a polymer resin which solidifies when exposed to UV light. It's broadly categorized as either *matte* or *gloss*, but which should one use and what criteria should be applied to the decision? Gloss lamination doesn't mark so easily and makes printed colors really pop off the page, so if you've got a gardening magazine or a book about color photography, gloss lamination would work really well. Alternatively, matte lamination feels contemporary so would work well on a cool fashion magazine, and it's very popular for quality fiction. The one thing to make clear is gloss shouldn't automatically equate to high style and wealth, as in a "glossy magazine." This concept is outmoded. **TS**

304

Thou shall learn the difference between embossing and debossing

Commentary This is always a fun question to ask any designer There's a good chance the answer will be something along the lines of, "Yeah, embossing is when the surface is pushed up and—no, hang on a minute—it's when the design is pushed into the surface and—um—err—bear with me while I look that up." I usually forget which is which because debossing is also occasionally referred to as embossing, not to mention blind stamping, so I always have to check before specifying one finish or the other. The correct definition is that *embossing* is where an area of paper or board is raised above the surface so it stands out from the background, and *debossing* is where an area is pressed into the surface to create an indentation. Both techniques require the use of a precast die, effectively an ink-free printing block, which is applied to the surface under pressure to create the shape. So there you have it . . . At least I think that's it. I'd better check. **TS**

Thou shall press for H&T bands when a hardcover is specified

Commentary H&T bands (head and tail) bands are the decorative addition at the top and bottom of the spine when a hardcover book is bound. A small strip of cloth with either a solid color or patterned, they are a small detail but one with a big impact. In the past, they were an intrinsic part of the binding process as the pages to be held together were sewn to this cloth strip. These days, H&T bands do not contribute to the integrity of the binding but are retained as an attractive feature. What I love about them is they really finish a book off, and it's these little details that provide beauty and longevity to a book's lifespan. They remind me of the traditions of bookbinding's past and add a colorful finishing touch to the end design. It may be that the budget doesn't allow for them but if you don't ask you don't get, so do always ask! **PD**

Thou shall always think about small details that create a big impact

Commentary One of the drawbacks of the computer is its inability to simulate special details. Gold foil, embossing, engraving, and die cuts exist in the three-dimensional world. As most work is done on a computer screen, it is easy to forget these small details. But it is these details that create impact. A book cover embossed with a gold foil sparks an emotional response and transforms the ordinary into something treasured. Engraved business cards may seem old fashioned and unnecessary. But in a world where most

communication is digital, a physical object is more important. The extra consideration of the feel of engraved typography begs the holder to caress the business card. These small details may be more expensive to produce than traditional offset printing, but their impact, however, cannot be overstated. Creating an artifact that will be kept because it has that little extra is true sustainable design. **SA**

Thou shall not specify predictable white endpapers

Commentary Being predictable is good for long-term relationships. Marriages with one partner who is loonier than a March Hare with wildly shifting emotions are hard to maintain. Predictability is good for cars. It is nice to know that the Honda will not break down in the middle of an intersection. Predictability in endpapers, however, is sad. An expected white endpaper in a book is dull and the loss of an opportunity. Endpapers can be made with a variety of colors and textures.

Endpapers can be printed. As long as the paper stock has the correct content and will remain glued to the book board, anything is open. The endpaper serves in the construction of a book. The endpaper, though, is like a theater curtain. Blank white theater curtains are dull. These send the message that the play about to be seen is not particularly exceptional. Or the theater is incredibly cheap and doesn't care about the viewer's experience. White endpapers are exactly the same. **SA**

308

Thou shall clean up the pasteboard before sending a job to the printer

Commentary This isn't a case of being overly fastidious with one's artwork (although one can never be too tidy!). It is a way of ensuring that the artwork handed over to your printer is not only precise and cleaned up but has no additional elements contained within that could cause errors or faults with the printing. Examples could be a lone text box that may have a text wrap applied. This could cause issues if accidentally moved onto the layout from the pasteboard. Another could be a linked text box that, if moved or deleted, could cause issues with the narrative or content. Again, images that are still sitting on the pasteboard will get packaged up in the final artwork when there is no need, possibly creating additional work for the printer if they are working on image files. The artwork is your responsibility, so keep it clean and precise. **PD**

Thou shall check that CMYK colors are not set to print as spot colors

Commentary I've encountered situations where artwork set up by a third party has contained many color-coded sections. However, not all the colors were CMYK (when they should have been) but spot colors. So a CMYK print job is set up to print with over 30 spot colors—an impossible specification! The problem is easy to fix and checking that colors are CMYK should always be added to your checklist as you finalize the artwork. In InDesign it's a quick action to highlight the color and switch the color to CMYK. Not doing so can cause confusion and possibly incur costs if a printer has to adjust your files. If you are supplying PDF artwork, and the problem has not been spotted prior to a digital proof stage, they will provide an inaccurate presentation of your artwork. Although most printers will alert you to the fact the artwork has not been set up correctly, save them the trouble and get it right yourself by checking first. **PD**

310

Thou shall learn about different finishing techniques

Commentary A printed object is a three-dimensional form. Just because Adobe InDesign displays standard double pages on a spread, does not mean that this is the only format. Paper can be cut, perforated, folded in unique ways, and trimmed to unexpected shapes. A business card can be oval, die-cut, or folded. A publication can have a cover that only extends to the middle of the first page, or folds over to create a gatefold. A letterhead can be trimmed with rounded corners. When appropriate, add scratch and sniff. This might be more difficult to sell to the client if it's a pet company, but perfect for a florist or candy store. Remember, the page, book, or poster is a piece of sculpture. It can be flat or as complex as origami. Unless you are aware of the possibilities, your work will remain flat—no pun intended. **SA**

Thou shall consider effectiveness against cost for special finishing techniques

Commentary I mentioned earlier on that, with certain projects, production and print considerations can play an important part in the overall concept. For example, two colors may be selected for the way they work together to produce a communicative result. The use of a foil block, a deboss, or a special color can also add real value to what you are trying to say; if this facilitates effective communication, then go for it. However, there is always a risk of creating "kitchen sink" design (one that has everything, including said utility). The addition of needless print processes does little to actually increase the design's effectiveness or its tactile qualities. If anything, it can often dilute or hinder the design, while definitely costing more to produce. I would always balance the intent and ambition of the project against the target audience and the budget. You'll find that the specification will be refined through consideration and a better end design will result. **PD**

312

Thou shall learn about PDF/X standards for artwork delivery

Commentary You'll have noticed the various PDF/X options under the Adobe PDF Presets menu in InDesign, but what do they mean? The first thing to explain is that PDF/X isn't some kind of alternative file format, but more a subset of the Adobe PDF specification. The idea behind PDF/X was to create a standard specification for PDF export which would help to eliminate common mistakes like missing fonts or images, and encourage the implementation of a properly managed color workflow. Put simply, each PDF/X standard requires a PDF file to match certain criteria such as compression, color conversion for output, transparency flattening, and so on. If you attempt to export a PDF/X file with incorrect settings, a warning triangle will alert you to any problems. The PDF/X-1a:2001 preset is getting on a bit and is less useful because it doesn't support a color managed workflow, so PDF/X-3:2003 and PDF/X-4:2008 are preferable when set against current industry standards for both offset printing and digital output. TS

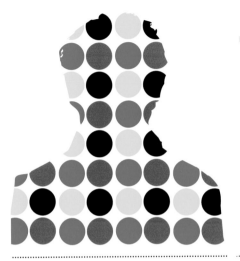

Thou shall not pretend to know more about printing than your printer

Commentary Everyone knows someone that hovers over the plumber when he comes to fix a leak, questioning every turn of the wrench and boring the poor fellow with tales of their own water battles, while he is trapped under the sink. That same person questions every car repair, wasting the time of all involved by debating knocks and pings and the cost of parts, until the mechanic's veins are bulging out of their forehead. Don't be that person. If you are a designer, you use plumbing, and drive your car, far more often than you purchase printing. It doesn't make you a plumber or a mechanic, and it surely doesn't make you a printer. Hire people knowledgeable in their field, be informed enough to express your expectations for the job. Then, let them do what they do best, just as you hope your clients will interact with you. **JF**

314

Thou shall not accept what a printer tells you is possible without solid proof

Commentary I'm very fortunate to work with some brilliant printers whose expertise and diligence make them invaluable collaborators. However, there have been many occasions when the supplier has been chosen for me by the client. Usually, this relationship is professional and productive, but, because you are not holding the "purse-strings," it can be a challenge to get the best results. Even though both parties are working toward the same objective—keeping the client happy— the designer and printer may not share the same priorities. This is where a little

perseverance goes a long way.

A situation may occur in which you want to make an adjustment to the artwork to improve its appearance but you are told by the printer that it is not possible. Don't take no for an answer: ask them to explain why and request some kind of proof. Only when you are satisfied it can't be done should you look at alternatives. Remember—if you are insistent, you may often find it can be done. **PD**

Thou shall understand the strengths and weaknesses of different printing processes

Commentary Every good team is an assembly of specialists (even if your specialty is being serviceable in several roles), whether it is in professional sports, a Broadway production, or your very own agency/studio. Some team members might be there to provide the big glory moments, while others do the dirty work, while others still provide micro specialties, the very best at a specific task. When buying printing, it is a good idea to think of your vendors in this way, to suit your various needs. In order to do so, you need to understand the nuances of the printing processes they specialize in. For each project, think about what you want to accomplish and choose the process that works best. Do you need lithography, screen printing, embossing, thermography, etching—the answer is very different if you are printing a t-shirt versus an annual report, or a business card versus the side of a bus. **JF**

The Practice of Design

Thou shall think of the idea before the visual

Commentary What do you do when you first sit down with a fresh design brief and a blank piece of paper (or perhaps a blank screen—more on this later)? Do you get stuck in with designing the grid and thinking about what typeface to use, or do you scribble away in a layout pad for a while to get the ideas flowing? I would strongly urge you to go for the latter option every time. All too often, it seems, designers sit in front of a computer and start on a visual straight out of the blocks without spending any time thinking about the *idea*. This isn't a great way to work because all your creative energy is immediately going to be focused on creating a visual around something which might not be the best solution to that brief, and an idea isn't about typefaces and grids. The visual exists to present and support the idea and if the idea isn't the best, the visual won't be the best either, despite all your efforts. Reclaim the humble pencil and get sketching. **TS**

317

Thou shall not automatically turn to design annuals for creative inspiration

Commentary I have to be careful here as I don't want anyone to think I'm out to dismiss design annuals. I love design annuals and as I type this I'm sitting with my back to a groaning shelf-full of the said items. However, the last thing I do when I'm trying to come up with a new idea to answer a design brief is reach for one of them. The problem with design annuals is they're full of great ideas that other people have already had. Everything you look at will immediately discount any ideas you come up with that remotely resemble the annual's content. That's a pretty frustrating position to find yourself in because there's no shame in coming up with a good idea under your own steam, then finding something similar after the event. It's a common adage that there are no new ideas left, which I don't believe is totally true but the saying does carry some weight. Try to look elsewhere first for your inspiration before checking out the ideas that have gone before. **TS**

Thou shall read books that are not about design

Commentary The dullest people are those who can only discuss one subject. Sitting next to the person who talks about her doll collection all evening is never pleasant. Dull people tend to have limited life experience, or they are genetically predisposed to being boring. Designers who only read design books and publications may be well versed in multiple design ideas and noted designers, but like the doll collector, dull. Design is about ideas. Almost any subject aside from design can be informative. A book on quantum physics may inspire a new way to envision information. Books about history can help us rethink proportional systems. A fiction book may be written in a minimal way and teach us to communicate more succinctly. Most importantly, books force us to question, have introspection, and reconsider our lives. If we are true creative people, this is not a simple, nice addition to our process; it is the core of a good process. **SA**

Thou shall not rely solely on Google

Q▾ for research ⊗

Commentary Google is a wonderful tool to search for a good local Chinese restaurant, 18th-century Virginia history, and software tips. Google is a poor substitute for actual scholarly research. Libraries are a better resource. A well-trained librarian is a human Google. He or she can help direct a designer to the correct area of interest. Searching for information on Google is like wearing horse-blinders. For example, a search for Cecil Beaton will lead to multiple sites about Beaton.

Some of these may be well researched and correct, others may be completely fictional. This search, however, will lead only to Beaton. Scanning books on the shelf of the library will result in accidentally stumbling on Irving Penn, Ansel Adams, or a multitude of other photographers previously unknown. Research is compiling verifiable data from multiple credible sources. A website about Beaton created by a fifteen year old for a high school project is none of these things. **SA**

Thou shall not *knowingly* plagiarize

Commentary The term "what goes around, comes around" can often be applied to our industry. Visual trends are created and followed, only to be replaced with a new theme a short time later. When these trends arise there is a chance that, with designers taking the same approach, work of a similar concept or appearance will occur. It stands to reason. On a few occasions I've had my ideas and work copied; while flattering (for a brief moment), it is also frustrating because all the effort you undertook to get to that end result has been "lifted" in a moment. So design for the brief and create your own ideas—that's the challenge of what we do and where the enjoyment comes from. It's being original that counts and this is what makes the successful designers stand out from the pack. Be honest and you will take greater satisfaction in what you do—your work will be appreciated more because it is original! **PD**

Thou shall insist on a written brief for every project

Commentary John the designer is looking forward to working with his new client and arrives in good time for the briefing. "Good to meet you," says Trevor the client. "I've looked at your website and love your work—it's so our kind of thing." "What do you have in mind for your brochure?" asks John. "Oh, we want you to decide as your work is so our kind of thing," says Trevor. "I'd really prefer some direction from you first so I know I'm on the right track," says John. "No need," says Trevor. "We love everything on your website." "Well—OK," says John.

Two weeks later John arrives to present his concept for the brochure. Trevor looks over the visuals, turns to John and says, "Oh dear, this approach really isn't what we had in mind. Sorry, John, but I'm afraid you'll have to start all over again and not get paid any extra money." "But..." says John. "No buts, John. It's that or we'll have to look elsewhere," says Trevor. The moral of this sad tale—always get a written brief. The end. **TS**

Thou shall ask clients questions in addition to the brief

Commentary That written brief is a real plus at the start of any project, but more often than not it can throw up more questions than answers. These can be many and varied but don't be afraid to ask them—just don't ask questions that are answered in the written brief already! What you will achieve by asking questions is to tighten up the brief, which will invariably help focus the client's mind and allow them to make decisions about the design, management, and production of the product. I often receive briefs verbally and take notes but again, there is always a need to ask further questions of the client. The obvious is usually stated, such as schedules and budgets (or sometimes not) but questions that often arise may include assignment of responsibilities between client and designer, budget structure, and billing terms. **PD**

Thou shall confirm all deliverables in writing

Commentary If you are working for a client who has commissioned graphic designers before, the protocols and division of responsibilities are likely to be well understood. But when you receive a new brief, it is vital that you put in writing what you will deliver and by when. I've often gone into a briefing meeting with clients who discuss the project with me as if I have a prior knowledge of what's needed. Of course, they have been discussing and planning the brief for weeks, maybe months, so a key task is to "go back to the start" and establish exactly what they require. Get the deliverables established and confirm with them in writing what they will receive so their expectations are met and there is no disappointment or frustration in the relationship. **PD**

Thou shall agree on costs in writing before beginning each project

Thou shall question a budget if it is clearly not enough to answer the brief

Commentary If there is one subject that is going to cause disagreement between a client and a designer, it's money. Clients do not like "surprises," especially those of the "project has gone up in cost" kind! So, to avoid dispute, confirm the crucial question of how much a project will cost. Whether working to a fixed fee or a day rate, make sure you have it in writing and get the client's explicit acknowledgment of the sum. In addition, if you are preparing a quotation, make sure that all elements of the prospective job are included: corrections; print management, meetings, commissioning of photography and illustrations, and so on. If you can't, then declare on your quotation that certain aspects of the project are to be confirmed. If the client understands what they are paying for from the outset, then all will be well. **PD**

Commentary Despite the fact that designers possess a creative side, and we all enjoy our vocation, it is our job and we have to make a living from our efforts. As such, there is no point in working on a project and not getting paid enough (or worse, making a loss). There will be occasions when a client comes to you with what promises to be an exciting project but with little in the way of budget and, as you read the brief or discuss with the client what needs to be done, it becomes clear that their expectations exceed their bank balance. Don't be afraid or unwilling to raise the issue with them—you are entering into a business arrangement and they are buying your skills and experience in order to achieve the desired results. I find discussing options and differing formats will often deliver a solution that works for both parties. **PD**

Thou shall not try to do everything yourself at the expense of a project

Commentary If you're a freelancer working for yourself, this rule doesn't really apply to you so please skip to the next page. If you work in a design management role or indeed as any part of a team, then please read on. This rule shouldn't be confused with Rule #245, which concerns commissioning. This one is more about being prepared to relinquish control over aspects of a project that other people can handle as well as or better than you. Delegation of responsibility can be a lot harder than you might think, probably because in the back of your mind the troublesome little thought that someone else's mistake might come back to bite you compels you to try to take responsibility for everything yourself. This attitude can do far more harm than good to a project and is unlikely to produce a better result. It's more likely to produce weaknesses in the areas you couldn't give 100% to and make you look like an idiot. If you learn to put your trust in others, they'll respond positively and generously. TS

Thou shall accept that every project will probably be more difficult than you expected

Thou shall accept that every project will take longer than you expected

Commentary Designers have a tendency to challenge themselves. We don't want to do the same project repeatedly and once we become proficient in one area, we want to venture into new territory. Therefore, almost every project will be more challenging than expected. Even the simplest projects tempt us to rethink and reimagine possibilities. If a person wanted to repeat projects without challenging themselves it would be preferable to take on a career in a poultry factory. The downside of the designer's need to challenge themself is time. Rarely does a project have too much time. A designer will work on something until it is dragged from his or her hands. A good rule of thumb is to honestly calculate how long it will take to do a project, then triple it. **SA**

Commentary I would really like to write more about why every project you ever work on will take longer than you think, but unfortunately my deadline for the submission of this text has passed and I've run out of time. I was sure I had another week to go before I had to hand this in. Oh well—just goes to show, doesn't it! **TS**

Thou shall dress for work according to your client's or your employer's expectations

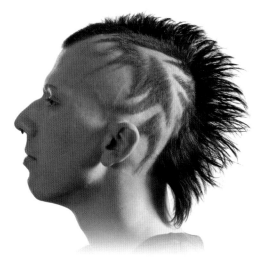

Commentary It is a mistake to believe you are dressing to express your creativity and that these choices only reflect on you. We dress to show our respect for those around us. If we are meeting with a group of friends at the local tiki bar, it is reasonable to dress for the occasion to fit in with the group. Wearing a giant teddy bear suit will make most friends uncomfortable. The same is true when meeting clients, or working at the studio. The clothes reflect the respect shown to the client or employer. This works in both directions. If a client is formal, and it is traditional in his office to wear something less casual, follow suit. Shorts and flip flop sandals are a not-so-subtle way of saying, "F*%# you." But if a client is casual and takes pride in her relaxed atmosphere, it is a mistake to wear a suit. The questions to be asked when confused are these, "What will make my client feel that I took the time to present myself in the best way? And what will create a comfortable situation for myself and others?" **SA**

330

Thou shall not present
an option you don't want
your client to choose because
they'll choose it

A. **Univers**   C. Bauer Bodoni

B. **Clarendon**   D. **Hobo**

Commentary It is an old maxim to never show a client a design you dislike. They will choose it, and you will be unhappy. It is a designer's job to solve the problem and create the best possible solution. Showing an unsuccessful solution is a disservice to the client and to you. Alternatively, if a client asks for a specific solution, do not ignore this. There is a reason for the request. Few people are simply mad and willy-nilly asking for wild ideas. Stop and ask, not how to visually solve the problem, but why he or she wants the specific solution. The answer may be extremely valid. You, as a designer, will have a better solution. But, never ignore the client and refuse to explore their solution. Everyone wants to feel important and valued. Nobody wants to be ignored and treated as an idiot because they "don't understand design." Explore the suggested solution, and return with this and a better option. Explain why one solution is more successful, not in design terms, but with an eye on the desired result of the project. **SA**

Thou shall be nice to colleagues working above

and below you as things can change

Commentary In Hollywood, there is a long-standing saying, "The ass you kick on the way up, is the one you kiss on the way down." If you are selfish, self-centered, and a sociopath, this saying alone should appeal to your sense of survival. If you are not a sociopath, you probably believe that most people should be treated with respect and kindness. It is easier to work with others when there is a feeling of common congeniality. Others are more likely to offer help and support when needed if you haven't abused them, or threatened to harm them in their sleep. This is especially true for well-known designers. If you find yourself courted by the design media, and climbing the ladder of fame, never believe your own press. You are not the best thing since sliced bread was invented. The people you look down upon and treat badly will remember these slights. They will tell their friends, who will tell their friends, and soon you will be a global pariah. **SA**

332

Thou shall not present reams of written research with a proposal just to impress the client

Commentary The teenager paces the kitchen, telling her parents all about the new safety studies, referencing quotes from other neighborhood parents, citing peer considerations, pulling out charts on mileage and fuel economy. Soon reams of information seems to be flying at them as she piles high automotive magazines and consumer publications; it is getting to be a bit much to take in. The plot seems to be firmly lost when

15 minutes are taken up with a bold discourse on how the color of an automobile reflects on its owner. By the time the kid is going on about how "if this car were an animal, it would be . . ." the couple finally raise their hands and plead for mercy. "If you want us to buy you this car, just ask," they sputter out. A solid idea only requires a little bit of explanation. You are not impressing your client, only boring them. **JF**

Thou shall not present mood boards unless specifically asked—and even then, under protest

Commentary This industry has a lot of dirty little secrets, and one of them is that certain agencies charge a lot of money to their clients for the pleasure of cutting up magazines and printing out images from the web to collage as if they were decorating their teenage school lockers. Originally conceived to provide inspiration by assembling the types of images, patterns, colors, and various items that a project should aspire to, they have degenerated into messy piles that serve as a bridge for clients that can't "see" where the project should be headed. If you read that last line, you will realize where the issue is. These are internal tools based on researching competing brands and the tastes of potential users/viewers. They aren't effective as a communication between creative and client, because your client should already know all of this like the back of their hand. If they don't, and request these, you might have a bigger issue on your hands than where to find images of "sunny teens that are smart and stylish." **JF**

Thou shall not work for free

Commentary As designers, we enjoy what we do. We mistakenly believe anyone could do our job. This is because we have a rare talent and cannot imagine everyone else doesn't. It comes so easily that it seems ridiculous that the person next to you at a movie couldn't tell the difference between Garamond and Bembo. Consequently, we give our skills away and devalue the profession and ourselves. There has never been a client with too much time and too much money. There are hundreds of important causes that need support. But often, when a nonprofit client approaches a designer and asks for free work, other vendors are being paid. The printer, caterer, staff, and delivery services may all be charging fees. As a designer, it is assumed that this is the "easy" job, and can be done in five minutes. Compensation must take place for the client to value the work and respect the designer. This compensation can be in the form of cash, goods, or recognition. But no job should ever be completed simply out of kindness without payment. If you are moved to do this, stop and volunteer for the Red Cross. **SA**

Thou shall invoice regularly and on time

Commentary One of the hardest aspects of running a design business is the business. Invoicing regularly and on time is more important than any other aspect of the business. It may be tempting to spend another hour refining the typography on a poster, but invoicing must come first. It is a basic in business to work with clients who pay their bills, and to invoice on a regular basis to manage cash flow. Some design firms invoice regularly once a month, but the most successful invoice weekly or daily. If a project is lagging, invoice a progress billing. Always invoice at the completion of each phase. Invoice outside costs immediately, even if this is a bill for those alone. Maintaining cash flow is job one. Invoicing on an irregular basis or late creates an atmosphere where mistakes occur and the client will perceive the design firm as amateur. **SA**

Thou shall not accept assignments purely for the money

Commentary For some reason it is a certainty that accepting an assignment only for financial reward will go horribly awry. There may be no logical reason for this. Perhaps it is the dislike and distaste felt for the project reflected in its solution. Or this is simply God's way of saying, "Do what you love." In addition to the immediate bad outcome, the bad project taken for money value alone will lead to other similar projects. Good people with good projects know other good people with good projects. If the issue is money alone, design is a bad choice of a profession. If doing some- thing hateful and only caring about cash is a goal, there are many other professions that accommodate this desire. Life is too short. A bus may hit you. No designer should spend his or her final moments before crossing the street, working on a hateful project with a disrespectful client. **SA**

337

Thou shall take days off—especially if you're a freelancer

Commentary A wise older designer once gave the sage advice, "Never work on Sunday." The point here is not a religious issue but rather a sanity issue. As a creative person, it is important to remember that downtime is as crucial and productive as working time. Taking time away from design provides an opportunity to clear the head and think of new ideas. At the least, time away from design promotes a balanced life.

Passion about design is important. Exploration and refinement take time. But design will expand to fill all time available. If a project has a deadline in 15 minutes, the project will take 14 minutes. That same project, with a two-week deadline will take two weeks. Unless you are doing brain surgery and the patient is moments from death, you can take one day away from your work. **SA**

Thou shall learn the rules before you break them

RULES

Commentary Many people have looked upon a vintage Picasso and scoffed with thoughts that they too could paint figures with pinched heads and wildly extended arms emanating from boxy shoulders. None of them are familiar with his near photographic early paintings, or else they would quickly realize that they might be able to make a rough approximation of the style he is best known for, but they would never have arrived at it on their own. Therein lies the difference. Picasso spent years plying his craft in the accepted ways, until he was able to replicate nearly any image with lifelike efficiency. He understood every nuance about how the human body was formed. He knew the rules and he knew them well. It was this understanding that made it so groundbreaking when he discarded them, manipulating parts and pieces as they never had before. His solid base allowed his creativity to unleash itself in the most impactful areas, forever changing the world of art. **JF**

339

Thou shall acknowledge your mistakes rather than try to cover them up

sorry! sorry! sorry! sorry!
sorry! sorry! sorry! sorry!
sorry! sorry! sorry! sorry!
sorry! sorry! sorry! sorry!
sorry! sorry! sorry! sorry!
sorry! sorry! sorry! sorry!
sorry! sorry! sorry! sorry!
sorry! sorry! sorry! sorry!
sorry! sorry! sorry! sorry!
sorry! sorry! sorry! sorry!
sorry! sorry! sorry! sorry!
sorry! sorry! sorry! sorry!

Commentary It takes a very mature person to accomplish this. I know I struggled with this early in my career. Couldn't I figure out a way to fix this without anyone noticing? Make it up to the client, or coworker, in some other way? I didn't want to disappoint anyone, or admit to myself that I was failing in some way. I soon realized that the best thing to do when you make an error, and we all make mistakes, so don't pretend otherwise, was to be honest about it. The sooner you come clean with your boss/client/vendor, the sooner you can limit the impact, or better yet, rectify the issues created. Everyone involved will respect that you came to them right away (as they recall their own mistakes in the past) and appreciate the opportunity to try to fix them as soon as is possible. Grown-ups make mistakes. They also fix them. It's part of being a grown-up. **JF**

Thou shall not ask someone else to do what you can do yourself

Commentary Smart people surround themselves with smarter people. Teamwork is important. Learning to delegate tasks to someone better is a key to success. There is a difference, however, between collaboration and servitude. Limited people find exceptionally dumb people and gracelessly force them to do menial tasks. If a task can be done well personally, then do it. If you are capable of pouring a cup of coffee, then don't ask the designer across from you to fetch it. If you have the time and ability to call a messenger, do it. It may seem fun and give you great satisfaction that you are the lord of the office, but this will only lead to dissatisfied and angry coworkers. Eventually, they will turn on you. **SA**

Thou shall find a design mentor (and be prepared to be one in the future)

Commentary If you haven't figured out by this point in the book that the world of design is filled with secrets, there is not much else we can do to help you. Well, I take that back, we can give you an important piece of advice, one that will lead to a lifetime of guidance. Find someone who has been through the battlefield already and form a trusted and cherished professional friendship. Finding a mentor can take a natural path, where you encounter someone more experienced and begin to ask them questions that grow into a tighter bond, or you can search out others via networking or professional organizations whose work you respect and begin a conversation. Ask as many questions as they can stand, but be prepared to fill the same role for a young designer in the future. **JF**

Thou shall remain humble in your work

Thou shall respect focus groups, but NOT at the expense of gut feeling

Commentary There is nothing worse than being trapped with a mediocre and self-satisfied designer. He or she is the type of person who will talk endlessly about his or her vast success and experience. By the end of the conversation, you will know their entire résumé in detail. You will understand that they are the most accomplished person on earth. The clear subtext in the conversation is that you are a loser in comparison. Every single person on the planet wants to feel important and valued. Charm is the ability to make the other person feel respected. Humility is a virtue. Humility is not self hate. It is the understanding that every person has value, and is needed and loved by others. This does not make you lesser. Reinforcing the positive aspects in others makes you genuine. **SA**

Commentary Focus groups have found their way into a bad reputation, in some ways justifiably, as they have been abused over the years. Having said that, there is a lot of value to be gleaned from direct feedback from potential users. If a focus group is selected properly, it can be vital to shaping how a product or brand can be positioned. Creatives are quick to chafe at the feedback delivered from these exercises, but take the time and digest the comments. There can be important information in there, and, if nothing else, respect the time and money put into the process on the client side. Now that we have gone through all of that, let's talk about the nagging feeling that lies deep inside us when we know we are on the right track. If your gut is screaming out to stay the course, don't let an unconvinced pool of people derail you. **JF**

Thou shall not quantify your creative abilities with software skills

Commentary Maybe it's an inevitable by-product of the digitalization of the design industry, but the average designer's résumé looks quite different these days. I'm venturing into angry old man territory here but when I first put a résumé together I didn't include a whole paragraph of stuff along the lines of . . .

* I can paste up artwork
* I can draw really straight lines with a Rotring pen
* I know how to blend Magic Markers with lighter fluid

. . . and so on. I kind of assumed that potential employers would equally assume I could do those things and I was hoping they'd be more interested in my ideas anyway. Fast forward to today, and many résumé include such a long list of software skills they begin to resemble a catalog for a computer retailer. Knowing how to use InDesign® is no indication that you're a good designer, so to be honest the information isn't particularly relevant, and besides, people will take it for granted you can use InDesign® because you're a designer. It says so at the top of the résumé you've just handed over. **TS**

345

Thou shall rest your eyes periodically throughout the day

Commentary The great designer Alvin Lustig slowly lost his sight at the end of his life. Nevertheless, he continued working, directing others to complete an idea. Being Alvin Lustig, it is fairly certain that his assistants followed his direction, using red, or Clarendon, or whatever he suggested. Many of us may not have the same command of others. If you were to lose your sight, you may request your assistant to use a yellow background and singular image of a beachball. He or she may then ignore you and create a chaotic mess with dark tones, but still tell you, the poster is yellow with a beach ball. To combat this scenario, it is critical to rest your eyes. Stop, at the least, every 20 minutes, and focus on a distant spot, or take a walk around the office. When the computer screen begins to seem blurry and dark, you have exceeded your viewing allotment. **SA**

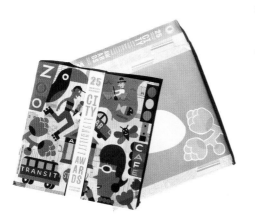

Thou shall work with talented illustrators, writers, and photographers

Commentary The single most important thing I have learned in my years doing this is to hire amazing people and let them do what they do best. I might be able to write, but I can't write on every subject and in every tone. I might be proficient with a camera, but others are so much sharper and creative behind the lens. I know my way around a pen, pencil, and paintbrush, but incredible illustrators inspire me at every turn.

People in all of these areas have shown the ability to make my projects a thousand times better than they ever could have been in my hands alone. Fight (and plan) for the budget to bring on the best, remembering how they lighten your own load, and prepare to bask in the accolades that an incredible piece will bring you. **JF**

Thou shall hire a good accountant and save more than you spend

Commentary It is not uncommon to hear a nondesigner ask, "I designed my own logo and business card. What do you think?" What can you say? "It's hideous. You're a sap. Are you brain-dead?" Of course not, but it is rare the result is anything more than sad. The designer who says, "I don't need an accountant. I know how to do this," is just as stupid. Designers enjoy breaking rules and play loosely with facts. These are not good traits in an accountant. Therefore, hiring a good accountant is a priority. And like hiring a designer, the accountant who charges a ludicrously small amount will probably not provide the best result. As a rule, always hire an accountant more expensive that you believe you should. The result will be positive and you will save money. **SA**

Thou shall build a team that complements, not duplicates, your abilities

Commentary Like a straw hat-sporting barbershop quartet, there is no need for everyone to sing bass. Surrounding yourself with a bevy of people that think and act just like you can be more than counterproductive, it can be downright creepy, like a science fiction movie filled with clones moving silently in concert with one another. In practice, it narrows the possibilities of how you approach creative problem solving and the diverse backgrounds and mindsets that you bring to your work. The chances that all of your clients are exactly like you as well seems remote at best, so a team with some range comes in handy at every turn. Of course, we still need to be able to work together and bond quickly, so be careful to build your team with complementary skills, not divergent mentalities. **JF**

Thou shall not be afraid to share ideas and collaborate

Commentary Keeping your ideas close to your chest is understandable if an original idea represents the difference between you gaining or losing a lucrative contract. If you're pitching against other designers (and not for free, I hope) the last thing you're going to do is turn up at the meeting and say to your rivals, "Hey guys, do you want to see what I came up with?" However, there are times when sharing ideas will win rather than lose you those contracts. For example, you've designed a brochure and your client tells you it's great and they'd now like to roll out the concept to their new website. Oh no—you're a print designer and don't do websites. It's time to go see the web designer that rents the office across the hall. The original concept is yours but what's to stop you collaborating with another designer with different skills to ensure you keep that contract? It's a good idea to have paperwork in place defining how a project splits before you start, but collaborative working is nothing to be scared of. **TS**

350

Thou shall get client approval on a visual before racing to finish a project

Commentary Deadline, deadline, deadline, I am haunted by this deadline. Balancing numerous projects is the hardest part of my job. The second hardest is figuring out this layout. Something just isn't working and I have been putting in long hours trying to bring it to a resolution. With the minutes ticking away, I am quickly running out of time to fix what is bedeviling my project. What was that hitting my keyboard? A drop of sweat? This deadline really is making me stressed. Wait, that's it! A photo of a water drop would be perfect. Inspiration just before the final cut off. I just need to swap out this illustration of a hose and then package my files and send them off to the printer and wait for my client to be surprised and be on the hook for the fees to change it back and possibly fire me. Oh, right, I should always get approval before finalizing a job, no matter how tight the deadline. **JF**

Thou shall not demonize another designer because you don't happen to like his or her work

Commentary Put things in perspective. As important as we say design is to society, it is, after all, only graphic design. A weak solution will not kill someone. A bad poster will not bring about the ruin of western civilization. An incomprehensible logo will not deprive your family of a home. Forming an opinion about work, and viewing it with a critical eye is good. But demonizing a designer who created a piece you dislike is foolish. Hating an evil dictator is a good idea, but hating a designer who uses a typeface you don't like does not set him at the same level. The best designers are those who remain open to new ideas and new ways of working. The worse designers are close-minded and rigid. These are the designers who wander through a career despising others in their own peer group, and truly hating younger designers. The tragedy here is the loss of opportunity to learn, grow, and create friendships. **SA**

Thou shall not discuss one client's business with another

Commentary One of the greatest joys in this business is working with people that you truly enjoy. Following a taxing project, you might find yourself bonding with a client over a shared childhood experience, or some travel mishap, or pop culture reference. Sooner rather than later, our favorite clients become some of our favorite people, and therefore, our friends. This means that we feel comfortable talking with them about just about anything, including what makes up the bulk of our waking hours—work. It makes sense; by nature of our relationship, that they talk to us about their work at times. Surely we should reciprocate. Talking about someone in the office that annoys you can be precarious enough, as they may be assigned to the client at some point. Complaining about your workload might make them think you are overburdened and they might need to send some work elsewhere. And talking about the secrets you are privy to with your other clients is the ultimate sin, surely going against your unspoken (or perhaps written) agreement with said client, and making your other client unsure how loose you are with their information. **JF**

Thou shall not criticize another designer in front of a client

Thou shall not criticize work previously commissioned from another designer

Commentary Consider this scenario: You need an architect to design your house. The first architect tells you how awful all the other architects are. The second and third architect does the same. You are left with the sense that all architects must be untrustworthy and spiteful. When we criticize another designer to a client, we do the same. We do not persuade the client that the other designer is bad, we denigrate the entire profession. The design profession is in a constant battle to be respected and understood by the business community. There are enough non-designers who berate the profession. We do not need to attack one another from within. This only reinforces the idea that designers are temperamental, difficult, and have questionable ethics. **SA**

Commentary It is tempting to sit in a meeting and complain about previous work created for a client. It may be true that the solutions are inappropriate or weak. It may seem that pointing out these weaknesses will elevate your position. Unfortunately, you may not realize that the work created was done in collaboration with the client. You are saying, without intending to, "You really don't know what you're doing." Never criticize previous work. Rather than overtly criticizing the work, point out some positive aspects. There is a good chance that the work may have good points, but doesn't work cohesively as a group, or support a new communication goal. **SA**

Thou shall never pretend you know more about a client's business than they do

Commentary A common mistake for designers is to believe they are omniscient. "What you need," they say, "is a new visual system different from manufacturing technique." Designers, like all other people, are not omniscient. A client will always know his business better than the designer. A client, for example, may be the director of a museum. While the designer has visited the museum and understands the audience and communication needs, he is ignorant of other issues such as staffing, acquisition, and security. Listen to your client. Clients typically have valuable information that informs the project. Don't be quick to disregard the client's issues and concerns. There may be a critical reason that you do not understand. **SA**

Thou shall be available to your clients at all times, but on your terms

Commentary As you sit outside the restaurant, with your meal cooling and your date turning to a frigid ice maiden, you listen to your client telling you how they just are not sure about this orange and maybe it needs a little more red, no, yellow, no, the orange is fine—you come to the realization that the line between work and the rest of your life has forever blurred, to your detriment. There is little purpose in pretending that a creative vocation means straight 9–5 shifts at the office. We are a service industry, requiring access to top decision makers, which means being available virtually at all times. Just accept this aspect and move on. But now, get your life back. Being accessible doesn't always mean being accessible immediately. Decide what is appropriate and work directly with your clients to establish this. Let them know you coach your kids on Tuesday, or that you will call them back in an hour when dinner ends, and they will do the same. **JF**

357

Thou shall actually talk to your clients— real conversations build strong relationships

Commentary People hire other people they like. It is more costly, timewise and financially, to find a new client than growing work from an existing client. A client will work with a designer over time and build a relationship through good work and dialog. Strong relationships built on mutual respect are more likely to withstand problems. When a project delivers late, a typesetting error is not caught, or a check is lost in the post, a strong relationship is vital. A long-time client is more likely to refer you to another client. Building this connection happens through honest communication. Take the time to have lunch with a client, play golf, invite her to a barbecue. These small touches build trust and make the difference between being a vendor or a partner. **SA**

Thou shall not discuss design with your client unless they express an interest

Commentary When your car is not working, you take it to the mechanic. Once he determines the cause, you want to know briefly what is wrong, how it will be fixed, and how much it will cost. Unless you are an automobile aficionado you do not care about the type of cam belt, spider gear, shift fork, or slave cylinder. When a designer discusses a solution with a client, he wants to know what the problem is, how it is solved, and how much it will cost to implement. Typically, clients do not care about complementary colors, the history of Baskerville, or letter-spacing issues. Talk to the client about communication issues, audience perception, and desired results. It is your job to know the fine detail. It is also your job to explain the decisions with language pertinent to business concerns rather than design vernacular. **SA**

Thou shall count to ten when a client angers you before opening your mouth

1.2.3.4.5.6.7.8.9.10

Commentary Thomas Jefferson said, "When angry count to ten before speaking. When very angry count to 100." As tempting as it is to lash out and attack a client when you have been angered, it is a bad idea. Rarely do we follow logic and give a measured response while enraged. It is not necessary to answer any question or respond to an accusation immediately. Counting to ten allows both sides to step back and hopefully find a rational reaction. It is more common to look back and wonder why you were so mad, than to feel that more anger was required. Another question to consider is whether the problem is about pride. Pride is a bad reason to engage in an angry episode. People tell themselves stories in order to survive. Let them, it costs you little. **SA**

Thou shall not accept your client's word as gospel

Commentary Clients only know what they already know. They are convinced that they need a small brochure and give that assignment. This is because they have only seen a small brochure and are determined that is the solution. Clients almost always give the wrong assignment. It is not the designer's job to blindly do what she is told. Your job is to solve the problem. That solution may be a completely different medium or format. Or the problem may be about the identity and not the brochure. This is as if the client visited a doctor and demanded a breast augmentation; the doctor may tell her that she has cancer, but the client would continue to insist on the augmentation. Stop and assess the situation. Step back and consider the bigger issues. Never take a reactive role and do as commanded. **SA**

Thou shall not continue to work for a difficult client

Commentary The only people allowed to shout at you should be your mother and possibly, if not violent, your spouse. There is never a reason for a client to shout at a designer. At the least, you deserve to be treated with respect and professionalism. There are clients who are challenging because they have challenging projects. But the clients who are difficult because they are abusive should not be tolerated. At best, they will refer you to other heinous and disrespectful clients; at worst, you will be demoralized and produce bad work. **SA**

362

Thou shall stick to your side of the project's schedule regardless of your client's input

Commentary This rule is a bit of a two-way street because it requires some positive input from both sides of the fence. Creative projects are always subject to change and as designers we all have to accept that it's going to happen regardless. Because of this, a client should, within reason, be made to feel that they can change their mind if something strikes them as important during the execution of a project. Whatever form that takes, the challenge for the designer is to still deliver on time and on budget, and I say again that changes would have to be reasonable for this to happen. On the other side of the coin, the client has to accept that not everything is possible, so it's acceptable for a designer to explain why a schedule or budget might not be met if a large change is requested. A reasonable client will accept this and may decide the change isn't as important as they first thought. Either way, stick to your own timing so late-running projects don't end up impacting on others. **TS**

Thou shall not procrastinate—ever

Commentary Procrastination is one of the most common bad habits in the world. It seems so much easier to put off an unpleasant task until tomorrow. The opposite is true. If you procrastinate, the task will loom larger and larger. It will seem more unpleasant and return to your thoughts repeatedly. The task will not disappear, so why ignore it. The solution is to simply buckle down and do the task.

Now is as good a time as any. It is much more pleasant and rewarding to tackle a task and complete it well in a timely manner. When you find yourself cleaning your desk for the fifth time while avoiding the financial paperwork, stop. Get to work on the paperwork. Never put off until tomorrow what you can do today. The pressure of guilt and worry will be gone, and you can engage in more enjoyable tasks. **SA**

364

Thou shall talk about design as an asset

DESIGN IS AWESOME

....

Commentary We often have trouble, as designers, explaining what we do to the outside world. Did you make the formula for the soda? No. Did you do the logo? No. Did you pick the brand colors? No. Oh, so you actually print the cans? No. Come up with the shape? Mold the aluminum? Put it in the box???? No. I designed the packaging. You can see how it quickly gets lost as to what we add to the process, though we all know it is the most important aspect. Design can be nebulous to the public, but also to clients. Boardrooms know they must have it, but they rarely know what it does. It is our job to be advocates for design. Make it clear at every possible moment that design adds tangible value to what is being created and is an essential asset. Speak in terms that the business world understands and stand firm. Design is important. They need us. **JF**

Thou shall keep it simple

"K.I.S.S."

Commentary The options available to designers to meet a brief are infinite, so the temptation to keep adding is very strong. It is important, therefore, to remember that the primary purpose of design is to aid communication and facilitate understanding. The best designs and the most successful work are always solutions that have taken a simple, clean, and uncluttered approach—the rules in this book go somewhere to guide you down this path. However, it can only come from you; the design process—as well as being ideas-driven—is a series of decisions taken by you to facilitate the brief. Make the right decisions and ask the right questions along the way and your ideas will succeed. Over-complicate and clutter your designs with redundant additions and they will be confused and unappealing. To sum up, in the immortal words of German architect, Ludwig Mies van der Rohe, "Less is more." **PD**

Author biographies

Sean Adams [adamsmorioka.com] is a partner at AdamsMorioka in Beverly Hills, California. He has been recognized by every major competition and publication including; Step, Graphis, AIGA, The British D&AD, and the NYADC. Adams has been cited as one of the forty most important people shaping design internationally in the ID40. Sean is President ex officio of AIGA. He is a Fellow of the Aspen Design Conference, and AIGA Fellow. He teaches at Art Center College of Design. Adams is the author of *Logo Design Workbook*, *Color Design Workbook*, and the series, *Masters of Design*. AdamsMorioka's clients include The Academy of Motion Picture Arts and Sciences, Adobe, Gap, Frank Gehry Partners, Nickelodeon, Sundance, USC, and Disney.

Peter Dawson [gradedesign.com] has nearly 20 years experience in the UK design arena and cofounded his practice, Grade, in 2000. He has won a number of awards for his work including ISTD Certificate of Excellences, and, most recently, Best Jacket/Cover Design at the 2010 British Book Design and Production Awards. He is a Fellow, and former Chair, of the International Society of Typographic Designers and has also acted as a visiting typography lecturer at a number of Universities in the UK and overseas.

John Foster [badpeoplegoodthings.com] is the Principal, Superintendent, and assorted other big words at Bad People Good Things. He is a world-renowned designer, illustrator, author, and speaker on design issues. His work has been in every major industry publication, hangs in galleries across the globe, and is part of the permanent collection of the Smithsonian. He is the proud recipient of a gold medal from the Art Directors' Club as well as a Best of Show from the ADDYs. Breakthrough projects for everyone from Coca-Cola to Hasbro, Americans for the Arts to The Nature

Image credits:

by rule number

Conservancy, ESPN to Chronicle Books, and so many more have established Mr. Foster as a constant force in the industry. He spends far too much time in his office, behind a giant desk for designering, drawering, and computering, with the world's goofiest foxhound at his feet.

Tony Seddon [tonyseddon.com] graduated in 1987, and during the following 12-year period lived and worked in London, UK, first for a multidisciplinary design consultancy, then as senior art editor for an illustrated book publisher. In 1999 he relocated to the south coast and has continued to specialize in book design and art direction. Tony now works as a freelance designer, project manager, and writer. He has authored three books: *Images: A Creative Digital Workflow for Graphic Designers, Graphic Design for Nondesigners*, and *Art Directing Projects for Print*. He lives in Alfriston, East Sussex, with his wife and his ever-present greyhounds.

Thinkstock [www.thinkstock.co.uk]

50, 89, 94, 110, 116, 128, 133, 137, 139, 140, 144, 146, 147, 153, 157, 159, 166, 168, 174, 178, 192, 193, 203, 207, 210, 216, 219, 220, 221, 222, 223, 226, 227, 229, 235, 236, 239, 240, 241, 243, 247, 252, 253, 260, 268, 274, 285, 298, 306, 307, 308, 312, 314, 321, 326, 329, 334, 337, 345, 349, 355, 358, 363

Shutterstock [www.shutterstock.com]

123, 160, 230, 231, 232, 238, 244, 276, 305, 309, 318

Vectorstock [www.vectorstock.com]

5, 92, 99, 143, 258, 280, 316, 362

Fuzzimo [www.fuzzimo.com]

344

Courtesy of Nikon

243, 245

Courtesy of LaCie

277

All other images were created by the authors.